JOB HUNTING AFTER 50

Carol A. Silvis

Course Technology PTR

A part of Cengage Learning

COURSE TECHNOLOGY
CENGAGE Learning™

Australia, Brazil, Japan, Korea, Mexico, Singapore, Spain, United Kingdom, United States

COURSE TECHNOLOGY
CENGAGE Learning™

Job Hunting After 50
Carol A. Silvis

Publisher and General Manager, Course Technology PTR:
Stacy L. Hiquet

Associate Director of Marketing:
Sarah Panella

Manager of Editorial Services:
Heather Talbot

Marketing Manager:
Mark Hughes

Senior Acquisitions Editor:
Mitzi Koontz

Project Editor:
Jenny Davidson

Copy Editor:
Sandy Doell

Interior Layout Tech:
Bill Hartman

Cover Designer:
Mike Tanamachi

Indexer:
Valerie Haynes Perry

Proofreader:
Sandi Wilson

© 2012 Course Technology, a part of Cengage Learning.

ALL RIGHTS RESERVED. No part of this work covered by the copyright herein may be reproduced, transmitted, stored, or used in any form or by any means graphic, electronic, or mechanical, including but not limited to photocopying, recording, scanning, digitizing, taping, Web distribution, information networks, or information storage and retrieval systems, except as permitted under Section 107 or 108 of the 1976 United States Copyright Act, without the prior written permission of the publisher.

For product information and technology assistance, contact us at
Cengage Learning Customer & Sales Support, 1-800-354-9706.

For permission to use material from this text or product, submit all requests online at **cengage.com/permissions**. Further permissions questions can be e-mailed to **permissionrequest@cengage.com**.

All trademarks are the property of their respective owners.

All images © Cengage Learning unless otherwise noted.

Library of Congress Control Number: 2010942046

ISBN-13: 978-1-4354-5909-0

ISBN-10: 1-4354-5909-1

Course Technology, a part of Cengage Learning
20 Channel Center Street
Boston, MA 02210
USA

Cengage Learning is a leading provider of customized learning solutions with office locations around the globe, including Singapore, the United Kingdom, Australia, Mexico, Brazil, and Japan. Locate your local office at: **international.cengage.com/region**.

Cengage Learning products are represented in Canada by Nelson Education, Ltd.

For your lifelong learning solutions, visit **courseptr.com**.

Visit our corporate Web site at **cengage.com**.

Printed in the United States of America
1 2 3 4 5 6 7 8 12 11

This book is dedicated to my biggest supporters—
Ryan, Niki, and Mikaila.

Acknowledgments

A special thanks to Mitzi Koontz, Senior Acquisitions Editor, for believing in and supporting this project; to Jenny Davidson, Project Editor, for her expertise and guidance; and to Sandy Doell, Copyeditor, for her insight and assistance. Working with such a fine team of professionals made completing this project enjoyable. Thanks also to the many others who had a part in producing this book.

I would like to acknowledge my supportive family, both immediate and extended, and the many friends who have encouraged me throughout my writing career. A special thanks to Sandra Hahn for always believing in me.

About the Author

Carol Silvis is the author of *101 Ways to Make Yourself Indispensable at Work* (Cengage, 2009) and college textbooks *100% Externship Success* (Cengage, 2009) and *General Office Procedures* (Cengage, 2001). She has had a dozen creative non-fiction stories and inspirational pieces published in national magazines.

Ms. Silvis was video interviewed in June 2009 by Tory Johnson for ABCNews.com and appeared twice on Cornerstone TV half-hour talk shows. She has also been interviewed for cable TV, radio, and newspapers.

Carol has a master's degree in Adult Education and is an associate director and department chair at Newport Business Institute. In addition, she gives workshops and seminars for schools, businesses, and professional organizations on a variety of topics.

Ms. Silvis is president of Pennwriters, Inc., a 440-member writing group, won the 2008 Meritorious Service Award, was past VP and Authors' Advocate, and was the 2005 and 2007 Conference Coordinator.

Visit her website www.carolsilvis.com and blog www.carolsilvis.blogspot.com. Follow her on twitter @carolsilvis

CONTENTS

Chapter 3
Using Technology to Find Employment 59

Chapter 4
Networking 77

Chapter 5
Attitude, Energy, and Dressing for Success 105

Chapter 6
Mistakes Job Seekers Over 50 Make 139

Chapter 7
Who's Hiring? **165**

Chapter 8
Create a Success Plan 185

INTRODUCTION

The good news is that companies do hire mature workers. The bad news is that many mature job seekers do not know how to carry out a modern job search or present themselves to employers in the way that best represents their background. Ineffective resumes, job searches, and interviews can derail anyone's job search, but they can completely shut out the mature job applicant. *Job Hunting After 50* will give you the information you need to carry out an effective job search.

If you are over 50 and looking for a job, you need to get connected. If you have not yet done so, you need to embrace current technology—purchase a cell phone, apply for a professional email address, and sign up on social networks on the web. Facebook, LinkedIn, Blogger, Twitter—these are just a few of the social media tools today's companies use. If employers use these tools, you should know how to use them, too. In fact, many employers use these sites to advertise job openings and to search for appropriate candidates. In addition, learn how to surf the Internet, fax or email a resume, and fill out online job applications. Once you do learn the latest technology, you will not be able to sit back and relax. Technology changes and evolves constantly. You need to evolve with it. Chapter 3, "Using Technology to Find Employment," suggests ways to use technology to your advantage.

Job seekers who are not comfortable using technology, especially computers and current software programs, are of little value to many of today's employers. Chapter 1, "What Skills and Qualifications Set You Apart?," discusses skill assessment and finding ways to gain or improve skills.

To attract the positive attention of an employer, be sure to have your paperwork (resume, references, and letters), appearance, presentation, and skills up to date. Lack in any of these areas could cost you a job opportunity in a market where applicants far outnumber available jobs.

Toss out the outdated, old-fashioned resume and bring in the new. Chapter 2, "Resumes and Employment Letters," will help you do just that.

In tough economic times, it takes hard work to get a job. You have to put yourself out there and call on all your resources, including family, friends, and former coworkers and employers. Chapter 4, "Networking," provides tips for utilizing the expertise of your support group and reconnecting with people who can help further your job search.

Over-qualified, over-priced, over-the-hill—these are negatives that can strike fear into a mature job hunter. Do not let these negatives outweigh all the positives you have to offer an employer. As a mature job seeker, you must maintain a positive attitude and disregard any stereotypes and barriers you are familiar with or have come up against.

It is not easy to maintain a positive attitude when you lose a job or are laid off before you are ready to retire. However, a negative attitude may hold you back from re-entering the workforce, especially when employers are looking to hire enthusiastic, upbeat workers. A negative attitude also causes a job seeker to become discouraged and give up before exploring all available options.

Your attitude is still something you have control over when you are out of work. You can decide to be positive and put everything you have into your job search, or you can decide to be negative and blame everybody and everything for your lack of employment.

Strike negative personal comments from your conversations, including saying that your age is an issue, that employers are not hiring, that you or your skills are outdated, and so forth. These comments do not solve the problem of finding a job. Chapter 5, "Attitude, Energy, and Dressing for Success," can help you adjust your attitude.

It is not easy interviewing for a job, especially when you have not been on an interview in years. In addition, most workplaces today employ multiple generations, each with its own set of ideals and ideas. Mature job seekers may even be interviewed by much younger interviewers. Chapter 6, "Mistakes Job Seekers Over 50 Make," provides insight into the multigenerational workplace as well as presents interview tips and techniques to help you through the all-important interview.

Chapter 7, "Who's Hiring?," suggests industries and types of jobs that are mature-worker friendly. No job search plan is complete without setting goals and formulating steps to reach them. Chapter 8, "Create a Success Plan," provides goal setting and action plan tips. Forms are provided so you can create your own personalized success plan.

This book cannot guarantee you a job. It can, however, give you the guidance necessary to conduct a successful job hunt. You can be sure the tips and techniques presented will leave you better prepared for your job search and well on your way to finding a new job. Commit the necessary time to finding a job, but work smarter by following the principles laid out in *Job Hunting After 50*.

CHAPTER 1

WHAT SKILLS AND QUALIFICATIONS SET YOU APART?

Years of working have given you an impressive work history that any employer would be glad to utilize, right? You might think so, but that is not necessarily true. You may have years of a certain type of experience, but if the job you are seeking excludes it, your 10, 15, or 20+ years of experience will be worthless to that employer. If you hope to get hired, you will need to give the employer what she needs. Find out the requirements the employer you wish to work for has by checking the company's website and reading its publications.

A recent scan of want ads and company websites revealed the need for these skills and abilities: organizational ability, oral and written communication skills, web-based technology, blogging, Peachtree accounting software, Peoplesoft, forensic accounting, logistics, SQL, MySQL, and Access. Depending on your field, you will need to know how to use some of these programs and possess some of these skills and abilities. Familiarity with current industry terms, software programs, and equipment in your industry will set you apart from other job seekers. Are you prepared? Skills and technical expertise are keys to landing a job. If you are not up on the technology or skills a particular employer wants, the job is not the right one for you. Desperately sending resumes to every company and every ad you see rarely works. Targeting those positions that fit your credentials and abilities is a better plan.

Even though technology is important, it is not the only job requirement. Companies today are looking for all types of experts in their fields who can deliver results that will benefit their organizations. The bottom line is "What does the company want and do you have it?"

Where is the demand for your unique abilities and expertise? Employers always have a need for experts in areas such as tax preparation, accounting, customer service, sales, medical assisting, home healthcare, and dozens of other fields. Your first step in the job search process is to match your unique abilities with a company that needs them.

What Is Your Purpose for Working

What is your purpose for wanting a job? It may seem like an odd question, but the answer will steer you in the direction you need to take to find the right position to fit your lifestyle and needs. If you want to compete for a rewarding full-time job, make yourself attractive to an employer through current expertise in your field. If you want a rewarding part-time position, you may be able to transfer your expertise to a new area. For example, some companies hire trainers to present workshops and many colleges are always looking for adjunct (part-time) instructors who are experts in their fields. If you are just looking for a paycheck or any part-time job for something to do, you can sort through your skills and abilities and match them to a position at any number of establishments.

Take Charge

To determine your purpose for wanting a job, answer the following questions:

- Why do you want to work?
- Do you want to work full- or part-time? How many hours do you want to work?
- In what type of environment do you want to work?
- In what field/industry do you want to work?
- What current skills do you have?
- Will you need to update your skills or learn new ones to be competitive in the field in which you are seeking a job?
- Besides money, what do you hope to gain from working (security, insurance, challenge, advancement)?

What Are Your Personal Assets?

Your background experiences will include the workplace skills you are currently using, transferable skills learned from former employment, and life skills learned from living. How have you helped past employers succeed? If you were successful at something in the past (for instance, solving problems), you should be able to apply that knowledge and outcome for other employers. Focus on the positive results you have obtained for previous employers. This in turn will shift the focus from your age to your abilities.

How proficient are your skills? Indicate whether you have a high degree of proficiency or expertise when specifying your skills and abilities. However, avoid exaggerating as you may be required to prove your claim during the interview.

Assess your skills, personal attributes, and special talents to see how they relate to the position you want. To jump start your thinking about your personal assets, look over the following table of workplace skills.

Examples of Workplace Skills

Sales	Analyzing data	Training	Assembling	Presenting seminars
Budgeting	Creating flyers	Child Care	Speaking	Software development
Writing	Problem solving	Coaching	Mentoring	Making decisions
Liaison	Team development	Evaluating	Maintenance	Production planning
Leading	Investigating	Recruiting	Painting	Dispense medication

> **Take Charge**
>
> Make a list of your workplace skills. Be sure to consider all areas of your expertise.

In addition to workplace skills, the various life stages of an adult provide an accumulation of transferable and life skills that could benefit an employer. Skills acquired from activities you have done for yourself, your family, and organizations to which you belong can transfer to a new position. For instance, raising your own children could give you the basic skills for providing child care to individuals or at daycare facilities. Someone who provided home healthcare for an ill relative could provide the same kind of care to other individuals. If you produced and distributed a newsletter for your personal business, that skill could be useful to a prospective employer who is looking for a company newsletter editor. If the last car deal you negotiated saved you a sizeable chunk of money, you could become a skilled company or union negotiator. Have you worked in a multi-cultural workplace? The global work environment demands that employees develop a cultural understanding and learn to work with people from all backgrounds. Fluency in a foreign language is a big plus. A good grasp of geography and customs is important to anyone doing business with other countries.

Get creative in matching skills with available positions.

Examples of Transferable Skills

Customer service	Handling money	Teaching
Filing/keeping records	Cooking	Demonstrating products
Running a cash register	Preparing bulk mailings	Maintaining appointments
Bill collections	Running a lottery machine	Directed work flow
Mowing	Ordering supplies	

Example of Life Skills

Maintain personal website	Blogging	Fund-raising
Party planning	Sports activities	Coaching
Tax return preparation	Repairs	Buying goods
Paying bills	Cooking	Cleaning
Child care	Budget preparation	Exercising

Take Charge

Make a list of your transferable and life skills. Include basic skills such as answering a multi-line phone, complaint resolution, communications, scheduling, and the like.

Round out your asset inventory by listing your personal traits. Include positive, current traits employers are looking for such as the ones in the following list that will portray you as an energetic, forward thinking individual and will eliminate the old-fashioned label mature workers often acquire.

Examples of Personal Traits

Energetic	Visionary leader	Critical thinker	Dependable
Tech-savvy	Coach	Innovative	Logical
Certified	Open-minded	Flexible	Progressive
Motivated	Positive	Loyal	

Take Charge

Make a list of your personal traits.

What Do Employers Want?

Find out exactly what employers are looking for and use the information to your advantage. Do an online search of the company you want to work for or request the company's annual report, newsletter, or other publications. Search for employers who court mature workers. There are plenty of them (see Chapter 3, "Using Technology to Find Employment," for the websites of such organizations as AARP, the Department of Labor, and the Occupational Outlook Handbook).

Look at what these positions require and what you have to offer. Is your experience relevant? Many want ads are technology heavy today, which means mature workers must have a working knowledge of computers and current software programs, especially web-based and Windows-based programs, to compete. Even the corner grocery store today is likely to use a computer to inventory products, and the local mechanic logs maintenance schedules and repairs on his computer. There is no getting around the value of computer skills today.

In addition to technological expertise and a basic working knowledge of business skills, employers want dependable, enthusiastic workers who will give a full day's work. Mature workers often must work harder to convince an employer they are skilled and physically able to do a job efficiently. Take an active part in your self-development through updating your skills and obtaining necessary training. This approach shifts the emphasis from age to skills and abilities, and from outdated to up-to-date.

If you are not skilled or need to brush-up on your skills, consider joining a professional organization or volunteering for a community nonprofit organization. Get actively involved and demonstrate your willingness to try new things. This will also show an employer that you are enthusiastic and energetic.

Remain active and exercise regularly to stay healthy and able-bodied. Manage your stress and get help for depression and other health problems that may impair your ability. If you have a disability, contact an appropriate government agency for job placement assistance. Maintain a positive attitude and demonstrate a willingness to get along with others. If you worked in a multi-generational workplace, mention your ability to get along well with people of all ages.

A concern of employers is that mature workers may be overqualified for a position with them and want too much money or become bored or leave if another opportunity comes along. To alleviate this concern, focus only on those skills the employer wants, not every little task you have performed in the last several years.

Take Charge

Research the companies for which you want to work and ask yourself these questions:

- Where is the demand for my skills and abilities?
- What is the company specifically looking for in an employee?
- What skills and education are required for the job? Do I have them?
- Is certification required? Am I certified in that area?

Match your skills and abilities to the needs of the employer so you do not waste time applying for jobs you have no chance of obtaining. Once you know what the employer wants, you will be able to highlight your most important abilities that will benefit him and subsequently make a persuasive first impression with your resume. (Resumes are discussed in Chapter 2, "Resumes and Employment Letters.") When you cram your resume with unrelated titles and duties, an employer may toss it aside or overlook the qualifications for the specific job he or she needs filled.

Make the best use of precious resume space by:

1. Thoroughly researching the company and position you are seeking.
2. Evaluating your background, including education and skills, work experience, volunteer work, life skills, transferable skills, and personal traits.
3. Sifting through this information and matching the company's requirements to your abilities to determine what to include on your resume. Downplay assets that do not fit the job description.

You want to include your unique talents on the resume, but you need to prioritize. Your assets that fit the position are the ones that you want to stand out on your resume.

Where Can You Obtain Skills?

If you are ready for a complete change from your current industry and area of expertise, determine the skills you need for the new field you have chosen to pursue. Do any of your current skills overlap with those required for the new field? If so, you might consider building on them as you acquire additional industry-related skills to solidify your background in the new area.

If you want to stay in your present field, keep up with leading edge research and developments. Read industry-related journals and newspapers. Join a professional organization and become an active member. (For example, Toastmasters is an organization that helps its members become better speakers.) Attend trade shows. Learn valuable software programs and technology as they become available.

Where can you obtain the training you need to enhance your skills or gain new ones? One of the most convenient ways is to take a webinar. A *webinar* is a way of providing training via the computer where participants sit at their computers and attend a live training connected to a trainer and other computer participants. Individuals can take part in the training as it takes place. Another option for Internet training is an online course where participants are not connected live during the class. However, the online class might include a discussion board with a live instructor during certain time periods. Both webinars and online classes are widely available on the Internet. An Internet search will display many of these classes, some of which are free.

Adult programs at high schools, vocational schools, and colleges offer inexpensive classes on a variety of subjects. If you intend to pursue a degree or certification, classes will be more expensive because of the credits tied to them. Check with your local colleges for a listing of their online and in-seat courses and programs. Some universities even offer information free on a variety of subjects like grammar, making presentations, and letter writing.

State employment offices offer free job counseling and training. Government programs are available, such as the Senior Community Service Employment Program and others offered by various agencies for the aging. The Department of Labor regularly posts occupations, projected growth, and the number of employed workers over the age of 55. Check to see where your particular talents fit or to determine what additional training you should obtain to fill one of these positions.

Internet sites are plentiful for over age 55 job hunters (see Chapter 3) and the AARP website provides a wealth of information. Libraries and community centers are excellent places to search for free or inexpensive training. Check your telephone book or do an online search to find these educational sources. Take advantage of any on-the-job training your company offers, especially if it has to do with technology.

Seminars and workshops are plentiful for a variety of fields and are offered by companies, schools, and professional organizations. They range from a few hours to weeks. Some offer continuing education units or certificates of completion.

Another way to freshen your skills or learn new ones is to study or train on your own through home tutoring programs, which include instruction in keyboarding, Word, Excel, and many others. Many office supply stores carry a wide selection of programs. You can access online training, learn from a professional organization, buy and use a self-help book or textbook on the subject, or find a mentor or coach.

Obtain training and information from reputable sources, especially with regard to the Internet. Do not count on the information on personal websites to be correct. Many of these website owners post information without reliable authoritative sources. Choose legitimate companies and educational sites.

Temporary agencies often train people in Microsoft Office Suite and other software programs when they sign up with their agencies. Filling temporary agency positions is a great way to earn money and get on-the-job training in a variety of positions. Temporary agencies may offer testing, training, and placement in companies that need your particular skills.

This is the age of lifelong learning. To stop learning is to be left behind and unable to compete with other job seekers. For every person unwilling to learn technology or current skills in his or her industry, another is eager to do so. To remain competitive and successful in an ever-changing world, the mature job seeker must change and grow, too. Make up your mind that you can and will learn the skills you need to remain competitive or to change career fields. Become a lifelong learner.

Take Charge

- List areas where you need to improve.
- Research where you can receive the training you need and enroll in a course or seminar if possible.
- Find a mentor to teach you an industry-related skill.
- Read a current industry-related journal.

Get an Education

If you are thinking of taking classes or going back to school to obtain a degree, develop an effective action plan. Talk to people in the field you would like to enter, and ask them for tips, general information about classes, how a degree could help you get a job, and overall guidance.

Think about the big picture before deciding which classes or degree you would like to pursue. Consult the U.S. Bureau of Labor Statistics at www.bls.gov to determine where the job growth will be in the next few years. Obtaining an education and a degree in a dying field makes no sense, especially when the U.S. Government sorts through the employment information and compiles a snapshot of the employment picture for future years. Research what industries are growing, where the jobs are, and which jobs pay the most and the least.

If you hope to regain employment or advance in your job, never take the attitude that you are too old to learn new things, especially technology. Flexibility and a willingness to learn will show that you are not an older worker set in his or her ways. Challenge yourself to learn as much as you can for as long as you can. Change and grow with the times.

Consider answers to these questions:

1. What skills and knowledge do you need to obtain or update?
2. Where can you obtain the skills and knowledge?
3. Will taking the class or obtaining a degree help you become more employable?
4. Will you enjoy the subject(s)?
5. Can you relate your current knowledge to the class(es) you plan to take?
6. Will the education help you advance in your job or career?
7. What will you need to change to make time for your educational pursuits?
8. Will learning new skills increase the likelihood you will obtain a job?
9. Can you fit taking classes into your schedule?
10. Do you meet deadlines or procrastinate?
11. Do you have an adequate support system to help you while you are earning a degree?
12. What resources do you need to put in place in order to fulfill your educational goals?
13. Are you motivated enough to withstand the challenges of going to school?
14. Are you organized?
15. Do you manage your time well?

Once you have an idea of the knowledge and skills you need and how they will help you, it will be easier to set appropriate goals and devote the necessary time to the education. Seeing the big picture and where you are heading will fortify you during difficult times when you feel overwhelmed or unsure of how to continue.

If you are unsure what education or skills you should pursue, online career tests are available to help you decide. A search of the words *career test* using Google or another browser will give you a number of these sites, which offer free and paid testing. One such site is www.careerpath.com, which offers a free career test, advice on professional career development, job satisfaction, skill access, and more.

Set your education and training goals in writing. Check into appropriate educational facilities, and make an appointment with an advisor to go over your plans. Determine the best courses to take and when and where to take them. If you are employed, ask if your employer will pay for any of the classes.

Learning opportunities include educational institutions, professional association events, workshops and seminars, reading, online classes, webinars, and so forth. Many websites offer information about finding appropriate online courses. Two such sites are www.guidetoonlineschools.com, which provides information about various online schools, degrees, reviews of school rankings, and educational resources, and www.learnhub.com, which offers links to schools, test prep, resources, and articles on education.

Think about all areas of your life where you need support and determine if you can get it. If so, put your support system in place and take advantage when needed. Who can you put on your list? Begin with friends, family, coworkers, former classmates, and members of clubs and professional associations to which you belong. Approach these individuals and ask if they would be willing to support you throughout your plans.

After you are enrolled in classes, take advantage of all the support you can get both at home and at the educational facility. For instance, if a grad student is available for tutoring and you need help, ask her for assistance. If you can complete assignments online or at home and save commute time, opt to do so provided you feel you will push yourself enough to complete the work. If you did not do well on a test or an assignment, contact the instructor for an explanation and tutoring. Can an established student mentor you? Can someone else at home do household chores so you can study? If you have children, can someone watch them while you study, or can they do homework while you study?

An awareness of your individual learning style can assist you in implementing successful study strategies and learning approaches. These are the three learning styles: kinesthetic (learn by doing), visual (learn by seeing and reading), and auditory (learn by hearing). Many people incorporate all styles into their strategies.

Because the way classes are taught has changed in recent years, you may have to adjust your notion of teaching styles. For example, in the past, lectures were the standard means of conveying information in the classroom. Today's classes tend to supplement lectures with more interaction, role-playing, team activities, downloadable handouts, computers, and technology, and other forms of engagement. Learners are involved in the learning experience instead of submissively listening to a teacher. Self-directed learning is popular. Learners take more responsibility for their own learning by making decisions, meeting deadlines, and working independently.

Whether you engage in formal or informal learning, you should cultivate a hunger for knowledge and pursue it throughout your career. A commitment to lifelong learning will benefit you in numerous ways during a constantly changing workplace and is an absolute necessity during difficult employment periods.

Tips to Get the Most Out of Education

- Be open to new ideas and learning.
- Appreciate what instructors and classmates bring to classes.
- Be tolerant of differences.
- Take an active role in your learning.
- Commit to lifelong learning.
- Face fears and counteract negative self-talk.
- Have the desire to learn and grow.
- Determine your learning style.
- Find a mentor.
- Relate what you know to what you are learning.

Take Charge

Decide on one step you can take right now toward improving or gaining skills and education that you feel will make you more employable. Contact the educational facility and schedule an appointment to meet an advisor. Start forming your support system.

Read Discriminately and Avidly

One inexpensive way to add to your knowledge base is to make a conscious choice to read widely in your field. By reading trade journals and industry publications, you will gain important information, learn about new advancements in the industry, and be able to participate in discussions with colleagues. With books and articles available on every subject imaginable, you can focus on information that creates value as you advance in your career or look for a new career path.

Be sure you are gaining information from credible sources. Think critically about ideas and facts presented, and sort the truth from opinions and assumptions. Look for accuracy, consistency, and quality of information in the types of things you read. For additional benefit to you and others, summarize what you have read and discuss it with colleagues.

Reading will enhance your vocabulary, which will then benefit your writing and speaking in many ways. It is not that you want to wow people with big words and academic terms, but you want to present yourself to others as a professional. A rich vocabulary can improve word choices, ensure use of correct terms, increase understanding, and boost confidence level. Add as many industry-related terms as possible to your vocabulary. Be sure you know the correct definition and spelling of words so as to use them in the proper context.

The benefits of reading include these:

- Increased expertise
- The ability to present the persona of an expert in the field
- Better comprehension of what you read
- Increased thinking and speaking skills
- Increased creativity and more ideas
- The ability to compare and contrast ideas presented
- Correct interpretation of what you hear and read
- Increased vocabulary
- Increased knowledge
- Increased self-confidence

Take Charge

Begin (or continue) reading trade journals or other publications in your field. Expand your reading to include books on other subjects of interest that tie into your industry or job.

Improve Your Memory

A stereotype believed about mature workers is that they are forgetful. Keep your memory sharp by exercising it with work tasks, games and puzzles, and exposure to new experiences. If you are having trouble remembering things, step back and take a subjective look at what may be causing the forgetfulness. A few culprits include stress, anxiety, poor nutrition, depression, poor physical health, information overload, disorganization, poor time management, and the like.

In this age of information overload, it is difficult to concentrate and remain focused on an individual detail, but there are some things to help the process. Eliminate as much stress and anxiety in your life as possible. Both distractions interfere with the memory. Get enough rest and stay physically fit to build a strong mind-body connection. Organize all areas of your life. De-clutter your mind by writing down details you do not have to keep in your memory, such as telephone numbers, amounts, events, dates, etc. Make a daily to-do list, and delete items as you finish them.

Prepare your mind to remember. Be physically *and* mentally present. Make use of memory devices such as acronyms, rhymes, and visualizations. Relate what you know to any new information you acquire, review facts and details you must remember, and share your knowledge with others.

If you feel your memory is lacking no matter what you do, you may want to seek professional help from your doctor.

Tips to Improve the Memory

- Eliminate or reduce distractions.
- Eliminate negative self-talk.
- Express an interest in what you are attempting to remember.
- Be observant.
- Link new and old information.
- Be fully present in the moment.
- Avoid trying to memorize important information when you are tired.
- Write things down.
- Use a to-do list.
- Reduce stress and anxiety.

Take Charge

Practice stress-reducing techniques such as reading, exercising, taking mini mind vacations, socializing with friends, watching upbeat movies, and the like. Use a daily to-do list. Exercise your mind with games and puzzles.

Gain an Edge

In addition to acquiring education and skills, work on increasing communication, problem-solving, and decision-making skills as well as creativity. Maintain a positive attitude.

Problem-solving strategies include analyzing and applying reasoning and evaluation processes. It is taking an active part in finding solutions while suspending judgment, assumptions, and stereotypes.

Problem-solving steps include these:

- Define the problem.
- List the facts.
- Brainstorm solutions.
- Decide on a solution and apply it.
- Evaluate the solution.
- If a solution does not work, repeat the steps.

Younger workers are often valued for their innovative, creative ideas and ability to see things in a fresh way. Mature workers, on the other hand, are often thought of as being set in their ways, resistant to new ideas, negative thinking, and burnt out from years of routine. Be the creative mature worker who dispels that stereotype.

Creative people are continuously thinking of unique ways of doing things. Because people see things differently, it is a good practice to engage others in brainstorming sessions and draw on their creativity.

Creativity can be developed by breaking away from routines and dropping the "that is the way it has always been done" thinking. Nothing stifles creativity like refusing to break out of the comfort zone. To get creativity flowing, shake things up a little. Change your habits, explore different options, and implement innovative ideas. Detach yourself from the ways you have completed tasks in the past and be open to alternate ideas.

Promote your creativity by:

- Being open-minded
- Changing your perspective
- Brainstorming ideas alone and with others
- Moving out of your comfort zone
- Trying new things

A positive attitude is an invaluable, essential asset in the workplace. There is no getting around it if you hope to succeed in getting a job or advancing in your career. Years of working in the same position or encountering multiple job rejections can wear you down, but you cannot let it show emotionally.

You will want to project an enthusiastic, engaging, energetic personality at all times. Making a conscious effort to be optimistic will help you override negative feelings and will attract positive people to you. A positive attitude will help you improve performance, learning, skill development, and relationships.

Turn a negative attitude into a positive one by

- Focusing on the positives you have to offer
- Focusing on the positives in your life
- Anticipating positive outcomes
- Engaging others enthusiastically
- Practicing positive visualization
- Analyzing positive self-talk
- Being happy
- Focusing on your successes
- Smiling
- Associating with positive people and avoiding negative ones
- Repeating positive affirmations to yourself
- Reading positive articles and books
- Persevering amid difficulties

What Concerns Employers?

In addition to your self-assessment, you need to think about the concerns employers may have about hiring older workers. You can then address those concerns while assembling your resume, cover letter, application, and portfolio, all of which are discussed throughout the chapters in this book.

Following is a list of some concerns employers may have about hiring mature workers:

- They may be slow doing tasks.
- Their skills may be outdated or they may not be competent.
- They may have health problems/risks.
- They may not be competent in the English language (or whatever language the company requires).

- They may not be familiar with the latest technology.
- They may be nearing retirement age and will not work enough years to justify hiring them.
- They may be looking for a job out of boredom and will treat it as a hobby.
- They may not have worked before and are unskilled.
- They may have poor hygiene or a disheveled appearance.
- They may have eye problems that prevent them from working on a computer.
- They may need time off for medical appointments for themselves or an elderly spouse.
- They may be unwilling to attend training and educational opportunities.
- They may have a know-it-all attitude or one of superiority.
- They may be unwilling to update technology skills.
- They may be set in their ways and become worthless to the company when it comes to keeping up with the latest advances.

Knowing what employers are concerned about regarding mature workers can help you figure out how to address these concerns before or during the interview. For instance, if you know an employer is concerned that you will be uncomfortable taking orders from a younger boss, you could mention you have worked with younger employees and are willing to accept directions from someone younger than yourself. If working with younger workers drives you crazy, you will have a difficult time fitting into the workplace culture of a company that hires a majority of them. If you know the employer is looking for someone dependable, you could mention your low absenteeism at former jobs and your ability to meet deadlines.

Your self-development and recent education, especially in technology, will tell the employer that you are willing and able to learn, flexible in your thinking, and up to date on the latest developments. Your volunteerism will show your willingness to go above and beyond, your high energy level, your ability to get along with others, and your desire to continue working. Your fresh, professional appearance will impress the interviewer and dispel the notion that a mature worker is old-fashioned and frumpy.

Matching My Skills and Abilities to the Employer's Needs

What type of position do I want?

_____

_____

Research for this position.

_____

_____

_____

_____

_____

What skills and abilities does the employer require for this position?

_____

_____

_____

_____

_____

What skills and abilities do I have that match the employer's requirements?

_____

_____

_____

_____

_____

Summary

Performing an in-depth analysis of your skills and abilities will alert you to shortcomings in your education and skill development. After analyzing the information, you will be in a better position to decide which steps to take to update your skills and gain new ones that will help you compete with other job seekers.

Researching the employment situation and potential job growth areas will uncover the best path to take toward your professional development.

CHAPTER 2

RESUMES AND EMPLOYMENT LETTERS

The resume is a vital tool used to secure an interview in the job search process. A well-crafted resume portrays the significant highlights of your background, including education, work history, and achievements. It is crucial to make a positive impression with a solid, targeted resume whether applying for a job by mail, online, or in person.

In addition, a well-written cover letter can not only gain the attention of prospective employers but can also afford you the opportunity to succinctly highlight your background and add information not included on the resume. When applying for a position, match your resume and letter closely to the company's needs.

The resume and cover letter provide the opportunity to present your skills and abilities to an employer and sell yourself as the best candidate for the job. They are your personal marketing tools to persuade an employer to hire you.

The Resume

Many people who find themselves searching for a job say they have never written a resume or they have forgotten how to write one. That is especially true for mature workers, since many of them have been employed in the same position for years, even decades, before they considered changing jobs or were forced to look for employment. Some may have been former business owners who dissolved their companies and had to apply for a job. Occasionally, a mature worker will be a first-time job seeker. In any case, not just any resume will do in today's economic environment and certainly not one with outdated content and format. Employers receive dozens, even hundreds, of resumes for each available position, and they spend from a few seconds to several minutes reviewing each of them. With those odds against you, it makes sense to spend the time to create a resume that accentuates your background in the best possible way.

As a mature worker, your resume will be different from that of an individual starting out in the workforce. You will need to showcase your extensive track record but not weaken your main focus by detailing every accomplishment and duty you have ever completed. Skip titles and duties unrelated to the position you want.

You may need to prepare multiple resumes for different jobs if the requirements are not alike. Fortunately, once a resume is created in a basic format using a computer, it can be easily changed to fit different employment goals and desired positions by deleting or adding pertinent details.

Resumes Then and Now

Resumes have undergone changes in the last few years. What worked in the past might have no chance of attracting an employer's attention today or help in securing an interview. If the resume that landed you your last job was written a decade or more ago, you will need to update it, and not just by listing additional history. You will want to use a modern format accentuating the outcomes of the duties you performed, using specific industry-related terms and those used by the company to which you are applying. You might even have to scrap your entire resume to gain a fresh, modern look. Read over the tips in the boxes that follow to learn how resumes have changed and what you can do to update yours.

If you have sent out dozens of resumes without results, consider using a different format or focus. For instance, you may be better off concentrating on your accomplishments and skills instead of specific work history.

It is always a good idea to keep your resume current even if you are not in the process of searching for a job. By adding pertinent information as it becomes available, you will avoid a last-minute rush if an opportunity presents itself.

How Resumes Have Changed

- The list of *work duties and tasks* was once a staple on the resume, but it is now being replaced by an *accomplishments* section of specific, measurable results.
- Employers expect to see proof of accomplishments—verifiable percentages, amounts, quantities, etc.
- Many companies accept only digital resumes (explained later in this chapter).
- Today's resumes should not exceed two pages, regardless of work history, in order to accommodate time-starved employers.
- Every resume should be tailored to a specific company or position and contain the actual words the company uses to describe the requirements.
- Although once common, personal information such as marital status, age, and health should not be listed.
- A cell phone number and email address should be provided. Include a fax number if available.
- Work history should be limited to 20 years or less of experience that is relevant to the job for which you are applying.
- References or the words "references upon request" are eliminated.
- Keywords (discussed later) are embedded in resumes.
- Often the objective is replaced or enhanced by a skills or qualifications summary.
- Area codes are included with every telephone number.
- In addresses, use the current two capital letters for the state abbreviation and no punctuation.

This chapter addresses the above changes and more.

Quick Tips to Update a Resume

- Eliminate outdated, irrelevant work history, education, and dates.
- Eliminate outdated technical skills.
- Avoid references to personal information such as marital status, health, and age.
- Use concrete examples of what you have accomplished instead of listing duties.
- List your computer proficiency and all the current software you can operate.
- Emphasize marketable skills specific to the job you are seeking.
- Keep it brief.
- Use a quality printer and minimize font changes and special effects.
- Include industry- and job-related keywords.
- Add a qualifications summary or professional profile.
- Use an attractive format that accentuates results.
- Avoid using a resume template. Instead design the resume to meet your needs.
- Use current state abbreviations—two capital letters with no punctuation.
- Eliminate high school education if listing a college degree.

Formatting the Resume

There are three basic resume styles: chronological, functional, and combination. A *chronological* format lists work experience and education according to date order, usually beginning with the most current and working backward. A *functional* format focuses on accomplishments and skills and downplays work history. Fields of specialization are highlighted with descriptions of accomplishments. A *combination* format combines the functional and chronological formats. Start with a list of skills and accomplishments and follow that with work experience in a chronological arrangement.

Before attempting to create your resume, write down your work history, accomplishments, education, and anything you want to emphasize. Then think about how you can present the information to lead with your best selling point. This process will help you determine what you have to offer an employer and how you can best get the information across so that it stands out among others. There are lots of acceptable ways to write a resume. Find one that fits your personal style and background and what you hope to do in the future. Margins, spacing, and layout are flexible, but the main focus should always be on the position you desire.

No matter what format you choose, arrange your information in sections such as contact information and special accomplishments so a prospective employer can see at a glance that you are fit for the position.

Be sure to proofread your resume carefully and perhaps have a friend or two read it. When you create the resume yourself, it is easy to miss errors because your eyes tend to see what they think you wrote. If you are mailing printed copies of the resume, use a high quality printer and good bond paper. Choose matching envelopes.

Digital Resumes

Job seekers must get with the times when it comes to creating resumes and filling out job applications by making them computer friendly. Companies, from fast food restaurants to retail stores to general businesses, require job seekers to fill out job applications on their websites or companies' kiosks. Typical company websites include information about the company's products and services, personnel, available openings, job descriptions, and salary.

Employers prefer to have resumes and cover letters electronically uploaded to their sites or emailed to them. Many do not accept paper applications or resumes at all. If you are unfamiliar with the process of applying online, ask a friend or mentor to help you. Learn how to complete the process yourself so you will be able to apply for future positions, which are apt to be advertised online.

In addition to applying directly to companies, many job seekers upload their resumes to online employment sites designed to help them find jobs (for example, Monster, Career Mosaic, Senior Job Bank, etc.). Employers check resumes on these sites and contact job seekers in whom they are interested. Keep in mind these sites may have hundreds of thousands of resumes so anything you can do to make yours stand out will increase your chances of having your resume read.

Formatting is a concern when you submit a resume online, because not all programs are compatible. To create an online or digital resume, eliminate special formatting such as shading, ruled lines, underlines, italics, tabs, or unusual fonts. Capitals and bold are okay. If the employer's software program is incompatible with yours, special features can become distorted when she tries to access the resume. Simple is better. Most company programs can read Word documents or Adobe Acrobat files, but it is wise to save your document in rich text format (.rtf) when you intend to submit it online to ensure it is readable by many different word processors.

Once your resume is saved, it can be uploaded to various sites as needed. Most company websites are user friendly, meaning they will guide you through the submission process, but you will still need to know the basics, such as how to browse for and attach the resume.

If you want to see how your resume will look when it is emailed to an employer, email yourself a copy.

Keywords

Most companies today store resumes electronically by having applicants email their resumes or upload them to a company's website. They also scan resumes sent through the mail and store them electronically. The companies' computers are programmed to find specific words (keywords) that match the desired job requirements. Whenever employers have positions to fill, they have the computer search all their stored resumes for those keywords related to the particular position in order to find an appropriate applicant. Employers can use computers to scan hundreds of resumes in a short time. If your resume does not contain the company's keywords, it will not be pulled up by the computer for review. In such a case, no one will ever see the resume or even know it exists. Therefore, using current keywords will boost your chances of having your resume picked up by the computer and ultimately read by a person.

How do you know which keywords to use and which ones are current? You can identify keywords by doing some research. Analyze company want ads, websites, and job postings to determine which words are used repeatedly in reference to the industry, and in the requirements for work experience, accomplishments, and personal traits. Read as much as you can in your field to familiarize yourself with industry jargon and the latest developments and also what companies expect of job applicants. Each industry has specific keywords. For example, a search for a medical assistant might turn up these keywords: medication, therapy, patient contact, personal care, medical terminology, coding, and anatomy. You would want to include these words in your skills, qualifications, and work experience sections of your resume and in your cover letter.

Do not create a list of random words as your keywords. Instead, use meaningful nouns and verb phrases that are key to meeting a company's requirements and to getting your resume in front of the person who is doing the hiring. Using a company's keywords sets you apart from others and increases your odds of success.

Search for words that describe the position and skills needed. Find out what software programs and certifications are needed. Keywords could be comprised of educational degrees and certifications, skills and abilities, titles, software programs, technical skills, equipment, industry terms, and personal traits.

The following list is a sampling of keywords, but it is not meant to be a substitute for doing your own research on the particular positions you are seeking. Use only the words for the industry and company for which you want to work.

Example Key Words

Managed information	Recruited
Lowered overhead	Increased sales
Organized	Coached/mentored
Analyzed data	Coordinated seminars
Created instructional materials	Project management
Strategic marketing planning	Visionary leadership
Researched	Global visionary
Staff development	Innovative
Interpersonal skills	Focused
Efficient planner	MS Word
MS Excel	Medical terminology
Computerized accounting	Customer relations
Problem solver	Team builder
Project team leader	Tech savvy
Fund-raising	Curriculum design
Public relations	Key contributor
Contract management	Negotiated
Purchasing manager	Inventory control
Budgeted	Statistical analysis
Marketing analysis	Survey analysis
Conference planning	Audited
Compliance	Projected
Human resource management	Demonstrated leadership
Drafted documents	Confidential advisor
Tax preparation	Accounts receivable
Diagnosed	Appraised
Mediator	Administered medication
Administered projects	Coordinated events
Promoted events	Generated ideas
Program delivery	Technology
Logistics	Quality control
Productivity	Capital
Cost savings	Efficiency
Instrumental	Conceptualized
Plan production	Launched projects

> **Take Charge**
>
> After researching the position(s) you are seeking, write a list of keywords for that position(s).

Creating the Resume

As mentioned, there are hundreds of acceptable resume styles, and the trick is to find one that best represents you to a prospective employer. The following pages contain the information you will need to include when creating a resume. This information is divided into segments as they would appear on a resume. Sample resumes are also provided.

To view additional sample resumes, read resume writing books at your local library, bookstore, or career center, or research the many online career sites specifically for individuals over 50. (A partial list of these websites appears in Chapter 3, "Using Technology to Find Employment.")

If you are not tech savvy or do not have access to a computer and printer, you may want to hire a professional to create the perfect resume for your situation.

Contact Information

Get noticed. Make it easy for an employer to find you by providing complete contact information in an eye-catching arrangement, perhaps using bold, centering, and a larger font than the rest of the resume. Include your full name (no nicknames), address (spell out the words Road, Avenue, or Street, and include the ZIP code), telephone numbers with area codes (including home and cell phones), and email address. In case you are not available to answer your telephone, the message for your voice mail should be professional in nature. You would not want an employer to access an inappropriate message.

If you do not have a cell phone, you might consider getting one to make it clear that you are in tune with modern communication devices. If you do not have an email address, sign up for one of the free accounts. Everyone in business today has access to email, and many companies prefer this method of communication even with regard to applications for employment. If you have an email address that is meant to be cute or funny, opt to set up another account using a professional name (preferably your own name) for use in your job search.

If you have a personal website and blog that are professional in nature, include them to showcase your skills. Prospective employers are likely to check the website and blog.

Objective

An objective is optional for the resume, but many employers prefer to see one. If used, the objective should specify the exact position you want or the type of responsibility you seek. Never use a generic objective; it is a waste of space and could hurt your chances of getting an interview if it is unrelated to the position being filled. If you do use an objective, keep it brief (one or two sentences) and tailor it to the position you are seeking. For the older job seeker, an objective is not as effective as a qualifications summary.

Qualifications Summary

A qualifications summary highlights your major accomplishments, skills, education, and personal traits in a brief paragraph or short bulleted list that the employer can scan in seconds. A number of titles are acceptable for this section, including Qualifications Summary, Profile, Major Achievements, or Significant Accomplishments. You may use both an objective and a qualifications summary, but if resume space is limited, opt for the summary in lieu of an objective.

Research the particular company you want to work for and tailor your qualifications summary to show that you have the abilities and skills required. Lead with experience and statements that draw attention to your attributes and successes, and use action verbs and numbers if applicable. Include industry-related keywords and phrases as well as those from the company's website.

Bullet three or four key phrases for your summary such as these:

- Skilled Administrative Assistant with experience in all areas of marketing and promotion.
- Confidential resource to supervisors and coworkers.
- Implemented code of professional and ethical behavior.
- Cultivated a high performance record of sales.
- Prepared and filed financial statements and taxes.
- Managed projects in conjunction with corporate directives.
- Excellent track record of providing customer service to over 75 clients.
- Proficient in MS Office, including Word, Excel, and PowerPoint.
- Maintained database of over 5,000 names and addresses.
- Developed a highly successful customer satisfaction survey.
- Integrated decision-making skills and good judgment to achieve maximum results.
- Consistently applied critical thinking skills.
- Versed in tax laws.
- Recognized as a team leader and coach.
- Interface effectively with corporate leaders and decision-makers.
- Successfully maintained 200-room property.
- Raised a record amount of capital in a short period of time.
- Set up and developed training seminars for company employees.
- Proven track record of decreasing expenses.
- Directed corporate educational programs.
- Interfaced successfully with high profile clients.
- Superior research, investigation, and analytical skills.
- Versed in all aspects of accounting and payroll.

For your summary, you may prefer to identify your qualifications and then show the results you obtained, such as these:

- Corporate Training: Developed instructional materials for a series of company seminars and workshops. Presented six workshops.

- Employee Retention: Increased employee retention by 88% through company-wide retention seminars.

- Employee Relations: Created training programs and trained all new employees. Facilitated workshops for existing employees. Motivated and coached all employees. Resolved conflicts and fostered positive relationships.

- Supervisory Skills: Assumed responsibility for 25 team members. Led by example. Resolved employee complaints and built team cooperation.

- Leadership Skills: Directed employees on policies, procedures, ethics, and communications. Held the office of president for local organization.

- Customer Satisfaction: Increased satisfaction by 34%.

- Personal Traits: Problem solver, visionary leader, tech savvy, organized.

Rather than a bulleted list, the qualifications summary could be condensed into a paragraph like the one below:

Demonstrated success by increasing client base and customer satisfaction. Solid track record of providing excellent service for attendees of conventions and conferences. Cultivated a positive rapport with event organizers and attendees. Maintained property at the highest level. Supervised a staff of 80. Recruited, trained, and retained a top sales staff and office team. Increased profitability by 30%. Utilized excellent oral and written communications skills.

Take Charge

Write a qualifications summary bulleted list or paragraph. Tailor it to the position you are seeking.

Accomplishments Versus Duties

The accomplishments section is a very important part of the resume where you can showcase your background, especially your education and work history. This section must give you an edge by showing the value you added to the companies you worked for that no one else did. The objective is to set yourself apart from other job candidates by proving your worth. For instance, employers are likely to hire candidates who have been successful at solving the kinds of problems they encounter. Cite examples of the outcome of problems you have solved and projects you have completed. Demonstrate how you can contribute because of your expertise.

When determining what accomplishments to include, ask yourself questions like these:

- How did you solve problems at your other jobs?
- What kind of leader were you?
- What special projects did you complete?
- How much money did you save the company?
- Did you increase profits or sales or productivity?
- How did you get along with supervisors, coworkers, and customers?
- Have you kept up with the latest technology in your field?
- Have you kept up with the latest developments in your industry?

Do not merely list duties and titles, but be clear about solutions you provided and what you accomplished. Show the prospective employer the unique skills and abilities you bring to the table by providing examples of concrete, measurable results without being wordy. Use action verbs, and bullet each entry. Whenever possible, quantify your achievements by using dollar amounts, quantities, percentages, time, and other numbers. A resume rich with statistics like quantities and dollar amounts will catch someone's attention faster than a resume without any numbers. Instead of stating that you have excellent supervisory skills, state that you led and directed a staff of 103.

Examples of entries include these:

- Increased profits by 27%
- Implemented cost cutting measures that yielded 15% savings
- Facilitated the smooth transition of the company move
- Supervised/trained 32 team members
- Presented 6 workshops/presentations
- Decreased shipping expenses by 10%
- Ran a successful promotion that increased company safety awareness
- Accumulated stellar performance reviews
- Scheduled and managed a staff of 30
- Exceeded previous year's sales by 12%
- Initiated a safety program that reduced accidents by 8%
- Led the team in sales with over $5,000 per day
- Operated an annual budget of $155,000
- Knowledgeable in computerized reservations systems Apollo and Sabre
- Increased customer satisfaction by 14%
- Developed a survey to measure customer service, which then increased customer satisfaction by 14%
- Completed 3 major renovation projects on deadline and 2% below costs
- Published 3 articles on insurance
- Launched a company newsletter
- Created a program to help the homeless that has assisted 14 individuals
- Analyzed sales data and compiled reports
- Expertise in research and analysis
- Provided coaching and mentoring to new trainees
- Responsible for generating sales totaling $500,000 per year

The idea is to list positive capabilities and achievements, not the day-to-day tasks you performed. Hiring personnel know what basic duties are required in certain positions. Tell them specifically how you performed and how that performance had a meaningful impact on the companies for which you worked.

Use action verbs like those that follow or ones that best describe you.

Action Verbs

Initiated	Recruited	Sponsored
Coached/Mentored	Organized	Assessed/Analyzed
Trained	Fabricated	Structured
Accelerated	Expanded	Supervised
Researched	Formulated	Instituted
Constructed	Produced	Demonstrated
Led	Inventoried	Facilitated
Expedited	Operated	Coordinated
Cultivated	Goal-oriented	Collaborated
Improved	Created	Saved
Wrote	Negotiated	Directed
Launched	Simplified	Upgraded
Mediated	Promoted	Investigated
Administered	Scheduled	Taught
Spearheaded	Raised	Achieved
Leveraged	Surpassed	Streamlined
Mobilized	Differentiated	Generated

Skills

List special skills and abilities related to your field that will showcase your strengths. Arrange skills in order of importance. Limit your list to skills related to the position you are seeking, but always include computer- and technology-related skills. Everyone needs to be computer literate today. Employers are always in need of technical skills and expertise.

Have you kept up with the latest technological advances either by using them or reading about them? Not being able to intelligently talk about technology will be a hindrance during the interview. If you are unfamiliar with current technology, consider taking a course or seminar. Of course, the best case scenario would be if you can use the latest software programs and equipment.

Problem-solving skills, communication skills, willingness to change, flexibility, and being a lifelong learner are all pluses for job seekers. They are especially important for mature workers who can be perceived as set in their ways and outdated by younger interviewers.

Remember to consider transferable skills and life skills when making your list (for example, customer service, sales, accounting, or presentation skills).

Key Skills

Internet Experience	Customer Service
Public Relations	Versed in Tax Laws
MS Office Suite	Recruited and Trained Staff
Illustrator	Research Analysis

Work Experience

How much information is too much information when providing your work history? How far back should you go? How will current skills transfer to a new position? How can you link transferable skills to those the company needs? What facts should you include? To determine the answers to these questions, scrutinize each of your past work experiences. Ask yourself, "Is this experience relevant to the position for which I am applying?"

The mature job hunter often has the problem of information overload, which leads to information dumping on the resume. This problem arises from the inability to sift through years of work experience, education, and life learning and then distill it into a workable resume. Many people who have been in the workplace for decades tend to keep things on their resumes too long. Having too much information, especially irrelevant or outdated facts taking up valuable resume space, does not make a job seeker more appealing to a prospective employer. Rather, it causes pertinent information to be overlooked and may show an aged, out-of-date worker. Brevity is in when it comes to resumes. An employer is likely to disregard a three-page or longer resume in favor of a two-page resume that contains key elements and has a fresh appearance.

How do you condense years of experience? Your challenge is to identify and focus on relevant skills and abilities. You want to interest employers without overwhelming them with your background information. Eliminate references to outdated and irrelevant software, skills, business machines, and education. For instance, not many companies use DOS or typewriters. It is better to limit these references to current company requirements. A research of companies you would like to work for will yield this information.

Today's resumes should be one or two pages of pertinent information related to the job you are seeking, regardless of your years of experience. Employers do not have the time or manpower to scrutinize lengthy four- or five-page resumes. A job seeker will be lucky to find an employer who will give his or her resume more than a few seconds' glance. Most employers do not even manually scan resumes. Rather, they let their computers search for the keywords discussed earlier in this chapter.

A young job seeker may want to list every little task he or she performed due to lack of experience. The mature worker, on the other hand, does not need to include mundane and day-to-day tasks or minute details. Instead, he should focus on major accomplishments and avoid writing a lengthy biography.

When preparing the first draft of your resume, go ahead and list everything you have done. Afterward, read through the information and cross out old, worthless experience. Go through again and eliminate anything that is not directly related to the job you want to pursue. Place the item most relevant to the job first, adding subsequent items in order of importance. If you do not know what the job requirements are, research the company to determine their needs. If a search does not reveal the company's requirements, research similar positions on other websites.

Instead of simply detailing tasks you have performed, show how your former employers benefited from employing you. Ask yourself the following questions:

- What value did you add to your company?
- How did you set yourself apart from your coworkers?
- How did you save the company time and money?
- How did you rise above your coworkers through promotions?
- How can you stand out among other job seekers?
- What expert skills and knowledge do you possess?

Take time to evaluate your background and determine what you should include on your resume. Read over the following questions and statements and write your answers on the lines provided.

- What is your area of expertise? Write down what you do better than anyone else.

  _____

  _____

  _____

  _____

- How did you become an expert? Write down the experience, skills, education, and training you have had and research you have done or written about that make you an expert.

  _____

  _____

  _____

  _____

- How did you take the initiative at work? Write down specific instances of how you took the initiative and added value to your company, coworkers, or customers.

  _____

  _____

  _____

  _____

- Write down a time you went above and beyond to increase customer satisfaction.

  _____

  _____

  _____

  _____

- Write down a time you met or beat an important deadline.

  _____

  _____

  _____

  _____

- How did you save the company money or reduce its costs? Write down specific examples.

  _____

  _____

  _____

  _____

- How did you increase the company's profits? Write down specific examples.

  _____

  _____

  _____

  _____

- Write down a time you coached or mentored a coworker with a project or task.

  _____

  _____

  _____

  _____

- Write down a time your problem-solving solutions increased your productivity or that of other company employees.

  _____

  _____

  _____

  _____

- What is the accomplishment of which you are most proud? Write down the accomplishment and specific details of how it added value to your life or to your company.

  _____

  _____

  _____

  _____

If you are creating a resume using the chronological format, list work experience in chronological order beginning with most recent. If you choose to eliminate some work experiences, try to cover the gap in dates with a statement such as, "I worked in retail and insurance for five years."

For each work experience, include the company's name, address, and telephone number, the number of years you worked there, the positions you held, and your major accomplishments.

You may want to separate the type of experience you have according to the positions you have held as portrayed in the following examples:

Management/Supervision

- Turned unproductive 200-room hotel into a profitable one, increasing sales by 30% in the first year.
- Monitored performance to identify ways to improve sales and reduce costs.
- Streamlined existing procedures and implemented new ones.
- Handled customer complaints and solved problems, increasing customer satisfaction by 34%.
- Assumed responsibility for 103 team members.
- Responsible for maintaining all facets of a first class property.

> ## Public Relations/Marketing
> - Created news releases for a 200-room hotel.
> - Launched a company-wide initiative to widen the customer base, which resulted in a 23% increase of customers.

Education and Training

In this section, list college degrees, credentials, and certifications if they are current and relevant to the position you are seeking. Begin with the highest level of education or the most recent. If your college education is more than 20 years old, consider eliminating the year the degree was awarded. Do not list high school if you have a college education. If you did not further your education, list your high school without the graduation date.

Educational listings may include the name of the institution, city and state, telephone number, type of degree awarded or certification, major subject area, and the dates if they are within 20 years. If you attended college but did not graduate, list the name of the school with the number of credits received. You may include brief details on the type of program or courses you took if they are pertinent to the position you are seeking. If you wish to minimize education, provide only the degree/certification and the name of the institution. Add individual seminars, workshops attended, and company training, especially if they are recent; this shows that you keep your skills and expertise up to date. Indicate the dates of recent education, including certifications. Mention all continuing education activities that contributed to your self-improvement.

Employers are also looking for credentialed individuals who have the specialized certifications they require. Keep all of your certifications and credentials up to date or consider renewing them if necessary.

Activities and Awards

List professional memberships, the dates you were a member, and any committees you served on or offices you held. Mention if you increased membership, saved the organization money, or provided vital support. List community organizations and any substantial projects you worked on and leadership positions you held. Add volunteer experience that shows your leadership, teaching, or supervisory skills (for example, coaching sports, mentoring employees or students, tutoring literacy students, chairing committees, and so on).

List company awards (employee of the month), community awards (person of the year), and certificates for workshops and seminars you have attended. Mention any special recognition, such as satisfaction letters from customers or clients and glowing evaluations. If current and pertinent, add academic awards and honors.

Include hobbies and interests only if they pertain to the job you are seeking.

Prove It

Show proof of your accomplishments through numbers, dollars, and percentages. How much? How many? What percentage? What dollar figure?

Do you have any tangible proof, such as articles you wrote or ones that were written about you? Have you received congratulatory letters and emails from supervisors, customers, or clients? Were you mentioned in the newspaper or in a company or industry newsletter? Do you have special awards or certifications?

In addition to citing these facts on your resume, you may want to put together a portfolio (discussed in Chapter 8, "Create a Success Plan") for your interviews.

Resume Tips

- Put the most important information first.
- Use action verbs.
- Quantify with numbers.
- Provide proof of your worth to your former employers.
- List top skills.
- List technological expertise, including all current computer skills and software programs operated.
- Be brief—one or two pages.
- Be clear and to the point.
- Be truthful; do not exaggerate.
- Proofread—avoid typos and grammatical errors.
- Tailor the resume to the specific position you are targeting.
- Use an attractive format; limit fonts and special effects like shading, underline, and italics.
- Use quality white or off-white bond paper and matching envelopes.
- Stress accomplishments rather than duties.
- Do not include references.
- Do not mention salary history.
- Eliminate outdated and irrelevant work history.
- Eliminate dates for education over 20 years old.
- Use keywords a company might use.
- Use a standard 12-point font.
- Use professional language.
- Provide complete contact information, including cell phone number and email address.
- Do not enclose a photograph.

Take Charge

Write a resume. Tailor it to the position you are seeking.

Sample Resume

Devonne Brown
945 Green Avenue
Pittsburgh, PA 15219
555-555-5555 (home)   555-555-5555 (cell)
dbrown@endnet.com

Qualifications Summary

- Corporate Training: Developed instructional materials for a series of company seminars and workshops. Presented 21 workshops.
- Employee Retention: Increased employee retention by 88% through retention seminars.
- Customer Service: Responsible for customer base of 150, an increase of 23% over previous year.
- Customer Satisfaction: Increased satisfaction by 34%.
- Administrative: Maintained a company-wide database of over 4,300 names.
- Supervision: Assumed responsibility for 25 team members.
- Human Relations: Interacted effectively with coworkers, project teams, all levels of executive management, and customers.
- Personal Traits: Problem solver, visionary leader, tech savvy, and organized.

Professional Experience

1994 to Present, TTT Company, Pittsburgh, PA, 555-555-5555

- Coordinated a series of workplace seminars to improve customer satisfaction.
- Developed instructional materials for various company training programs.
- Launched a company-wide initiative to increase the customer base, which resulted in a 23% increase.
- Maintained a customer base of 150, an increase of 23% over previous year.

Devonne Brown
Page 2

- Increased customer satisfaction by 34%.
- Interacted effectively to lead a team of 25; scheduled, supervised, coached.
- Managed information that was disseminated to all plants and offices.
- Maintained and analyzed a company-wide database of over 4,300 names.
- Coached and mentored employees.
- Created and disseminated information through corporate training seminars that increased employee retention by 88%.

1990-1994, Braids, Pittsburgh, PA, 555-555-5555

- Collaborated effectively with all levels of senior management.
- Maintained database of 5,000 names and addresses.
- Built a client base of 63 from scratch.
- Inventoried products, maintained and replenished stock using company-developed computer program.

Education

Received a Bachelor's Degree from the University of Pittsburgh.

Received a Master's Degree in Adult Education from Penn State University.

Achievements and Organizations

Member of Pittsburgh Chamber of Commerce, awarded Employee of the Month at TTT, received several customer satisfaction letters and glowing work evaluations. Volunteered for three years at a local food bank and a women's shelter.

Received six certificates for various instructional training seminars.

Sample Resume

Devonne Brown

945 Green Avenue
Pittsburgh, PA 15219
555-555-5555 (home)   555-555-5555 (cell)
dbrown@endnet.com

Expertise

- Visionary Leader
- Supervisor/Coach
- Communication/Interpersonal Skills
- Organizing
- Problem Solving/Conflict Resolution
- Project Management
- MS Office 2010
- Coordinated Seminars

Professional Experience

1994 to Present, TTT Company, Pittsburgh, PA, 555-555-5555

- Developed instructional materials for a series of company seminars and workshops. Presented 21 workshops.
- Increased employee retention by 88% through retention seminars.
- Coordinated a series of workplace seminars to improve customer satisfaction.
- Developed instructional materials for various company training programs.
- Launched a company-wide initiative to increase the customer base, which resulted in a 23% increase.
- Maintained a customer base of 150, an increase of 23% over previous year.
- Increased customer satisfaction by 34%.
- Interacted effectively to lead a team of 25; scheduled, supervised, coached.
- Managed information that was disseminated to all plants and offices.
- Maintained and analyzed a company-wide database of over 4,300 names.

Devonne Brown
Page 2

- Coached and mentored employees.
- Interacted effectively with coworkers, project teams, all levels of executive management, and customers.
- Created and disseminated information through corporate training seminars that increased employee retention by 88%.

1990-1994, Braids, Pittsburgh, PA, 555-555-5555

- Collaborated effectively with all levels of senior management.
- Maintained database of 5,000 names and addresses.
- Built a client base of 63 from scratch.
- Inventoried products, maintained and replenished stock using company-developed computer program.

Education

Received a Bachelor's Degree from the University of Pittsburgh.

Received a Master's Degree in Adult Education from Penn State University.

Achievements and Organizations

Member of Pittsburgh Chamber of Commerce, awarded Employee of the Month at TTT, received several customer satisfaction letters and glowing work evaluations. Volunteered for three years at a local food bank and a women's shelter.

Received six certificates for various instructional training seminars.

Sample Resume

Quentin Greer

555 Street Avenue
Pittsburgh, PA 15219
555-555-5555 (home)   555-555-5555 (cell)
quentin.greer@endnet.com

Key Management Strengths

Marketing Strategies   Customer Satisfaction
Visionary Leader   Dynamic Presenter
Coach/Mentor   Multimillion Dollar Budget
Research/Analysis   Problem Solver
Tech savvy

Significant Accomplishments

Demonstrated success by increasing customer base and overall customer satisfaction. Solid track record of providing excellent service for convention and conference attendees and maintaining a positive rapport with event organizers. Maintained property at highest level. Managed a staff of 103 full- and part-time workers. Recruited, trained, and retained a top sales staff and office team. Initiated new competitive pricing that increased profitability by 30%. Utilized excellent oral and written communications skills. Interacted effectively with coworkers, project teams, all levels of executive management, and customers.

Specialized Skills

Proficient in MS Office 2010, including Word, Excel, and PowerPoint; Internet savvy; website maintenance; Hotel Pittsburgh Software.

Professional Experience

2004 to Present, Hotel Pittsburgh, Pittsburgh, PA, General Manager

- Turned unproductive 200-room hotel into a profitable one, increasing sales by 30% in the first year.

- Launched a company-wide initiative to widen the customer base, which resulted in a 23% increase.

- Monitored performance to identify ways to improve sales and reduce costs.

- Streamlined existing procedures and implemented new ones.

- Handled customer complaints and solved problems, increasing customer satisfaction by 34%.

Quentin Greer
Page 2

- Maintained a company-wide database of over 4,300 names.
- Assumed responsibility for 103 team members.
- Responsible for maintaining all facets of a first-class property.

1999-2004, Dunnington Motel, Monroeville, PA, Night Manager

- Responsible for maintaining all aspects of 55-room motel including daily operations and upkeep.
- Trained and supervised a staff of 33.
- Maintained property records, prepared payroll, and built and maintained databases.

1990-1999, Basics, Inc., Pittsburgh, PA, Sales Manager

- Directed and led 2 assistant managers and 5-8 sales associates.
- Turned unproductive store into a profitable one; consistently met sales and profit goals; developed and implemented strategies to meet cost control goals.
- Prepared management reports.
- Hired, trained, and scheduled all personnel.
- Did inventory control and placed orders for fast moving merchandise.
- Monitored performance to identify ways to improve sales and reduce costs.
- Responsible for visual merchandising of the store, including wall and window displays and floor moves.

Education

Received a Bachelor's Degree from the University of Pittsburgh.

Certification in Hotel Management.

Sales Training Seminars.

Achievements and Organizations

Member of Pittsburgh Chamber of Commerce and National Association of Sales Professionals, awarded Salesperson of the Year and Employee of the Year, received multiple Employee of the Month awards, received several customer satisfaction letters and glowing work evaluations, awarded Salesman of the Month several times.

Reference Sheet

A reference sheet lists people who will provide a prospective employer with verification of your work history or education. References may be required after you have interviewed for a job. Do not list references on the resume, but rather on a separate sheet of paper. The reference sheet is not sent with the resume except at the interviewer's request.

For professional references, choose three to five individuals who will vouch for your work ethic and/or education. These should be people who will give a favorable account of your background. References might be former employers, supervisors, instructors, coworkers, classmates, and professionals you deal with on a regular basis. You may include one or two personal references if you choose, but avoid relatives unless you worked for them.

At the top of the reference sheet, place the same contact information that is on your resume: your name, address, telephone numbers, and email address. List each reference with the name, title, company name and address, and company phone number. If the reference is no longer working, you may include the words *former* or *retired* in parentheses after the name or title. In such cases, use the individual's personal contact information if appropriate.

Ask references if you may use their names before listing them. You may have to refresh the person's memory of when and how you knew him if it has been a number of years since you have had contact.

Reference sheet formats vary.

Tips for References

- Provide your complete contact information.
- Provide complete contact information for each reference.
- Choose three to five professional references.
- Contact references to ask permission prior to using their names.
- Print the references on white or off-white quality bond paper that matches your resume and mail in matching envelopes.

Take Charge

Write a reference sheet with at least three professional references.

Sample Reference Sheet

**References
of
Devonne Brown**

945 Green Avenue
Pittsburgh, PA 15219
555-555-5555 (home)   555-555-5555 (cell)
dbrown@endnet.com

Doreen Bolenz, CEO
TTT Company
Pittsburgh, PA 15219
555-555-5555, Ext. 108

Boris Constantino, General Manager
TTT Company
Pittsburgh, PA 15219
555-555-5555, Ext. 320

Margarita Lorenz
Attorney-at-Law
Lorenz and Ogdon
Pittsburgh, PA 15222
555-555-5555

David Bartolla, Manager
Bartolla Management
Pittsburgh, PA 15219
555-555-5555

Sample Reference Sheet

References
of
Quentin Greer

555 Street Avenue
Pittsburgh, PA 15219
555-555-5555 (home)   555-555-5555 (cell)
quentin.greer@endnet.com

Sheila Davis
Manager
Basics, Inc.
555 Basics St.
Pittsburgh, PA 15219
555-555-5555

Tom Smith
Attorney-at-Law
555 Smith St
Pittsburgh, PA 15219
555-555-5555

Harry Edwards
Hotel Pittsburgh
111 Street Ave.
Pittsburgh, PA 15219
555-555-5555

Susan Thomas
Manager
Dunnington Motel
Monroeville, PA 15555
555-555-5555

Cover Letter

A cover letter is a must for every resume mailed or faxed. A cover letter is also recommended when submitting resumes online or on company websites. A well-written cover letter can give you an edge by grabbing the prospective employer's attention. It also gives you a chance to expand on information not appropriate for the resume such as salary history or relevant hobbies and interests. Keeping the purpose of your letter in mind (to gain an interview), outline your strongest qualities that match the job for which you are applying. The letter should be tailored to the position and be addressed to a specific person, using the person's correct title and business address. If you do not have a specific position or a contact name, then research the company's website to find appropriate positions and personnel.

Use keywords from the company's website or want ad. To keep from seeming out of date, reference current technology and industry developments, and avoid the old-fashioned expressions and terms. Never use the salutation *To Whom It May Concern*. If you do not have a specific name to address in your letter, use the salutation *Hiring Manager*. Never photocopy a generic letter. Compose a fresh letter for each job to which you apply.

The initial paragraph of your cover letter should open with a sentence to grab the reader's attention. Get to the point by indicating your interest in a position and how you heard of it. Succinctly summarize your most impressive credentials. Focus on what you can do for the company. If someone recommended that you apply for the position, use the person's name in the opening sentence.

The middle paragraph(s) presents background information such as work history, education and certifications, accomplishments, personal characteristics, and your qualifications for the position. Do not re-copy information from your resume; rather, highlight the important parts. Describe how your abilities match the company's requirements and provide evidence of how you can fill those requirements. You must address the needs of the company, not your needs. Mention that the resume is enclosed.

In the final paragraph, request an interview to discuss your qualifications and how they can benefit the prospective employer. Include contact information and your availability in this paragraph. You might also state your intention to follow up your letter with a telephone call. Express your appreciation.

To strengthen the cover letter, use action verbs, match your qualifications to the needs of the company, use an appropriate format and high-quality paper that matches your resume. Proofread, and sign your name. Fold the letter and resume together, but do not paperclip or staple the documents.

Tips for Writing a Cover Letter

- Use proper letter format.
- Provide your contact information.
- Use high-quality white or off-white bond paper to match the resume.
- Use keywords and terms relevant to the job you are seeking.
- Tailor the letter to a specific position.
- Be specific and clear.
- Be brief, but give complete information.
- Avoid out-dated language.
- Address the letter to a specific person.
- Request an interview.
- Make reference to your enclosed resume.
- Give concrete examples of your accomplishments.
- If referred by someone, state the person's name in the first sentence.
- Break information into logical paragraphs.
- Double check dates, names, and addresses.
- Proofread carefully.
- Sign the letter in ink.

Take Charge

Write a cover letter. Tailor it to the position you are seeking.

Sample Cover Letter

Devonne Brown
945 Green Avenue   Pittsburgh, PA 15219
555-555-5555 (home)   555-555-5555 (cell)   dbrown@endnet.com

(Current Date)

Hiring Manager:

Travis DeWitt suggested I contact you regarding the position of Learning and Development Training Specialist with XYZ Company. Please consider my application. Providing training for over 300 employees has given me an edge when it comes to dealing with adults and their individual styles. My experience involves working with a wide variety of personalities.

I am on top of developments in my field because of research for my publications and presentations. I recently created an Emergency Incident Response Policy for TTT Company.

My skills and qualifications closely align with the requirements and criteria you are looking for in this position. Here is an overview of my administrative and teaching background:

- Develop and update materials for training presentations according to company procedures and policies.
- Evaluated, coached, and mentored over 130 employees.
- Organize staff development.
- Assist with long-term planning for company training programs.

In addition to working full-time, I coordinated two conferences for an association of over 500 members to which I belong. I handled all aspects of the conferences, and arranged speakers from across the US, airline flights, hotel rooms, meal selections, and workshops. I created conference brochures, programs, evaluation forms, and other documentation. In addition, I coordinated a community day where over 20 presenters disseminated information to hundreds of community members.

Please review my resume detailing my education and professional experience. I would be happy to meet with you and discuss my qualifications further.

Sincerely yours,

Devonne Brown
Enclosure

Sample Cover Letter

Devonne Brown
945 Green Avenue
Pittsburgh, PA 15219
555-555-5555 (home)   555-555-5555 (cell)
dbrown@endnet.com

(Current date)

Stanley Gonzore
XARR Corporation
999 Bentley Avenue
Pittsburgh, PA 15222

Dear Mr. Gonzore:

Please consider me an applicant for the Compliance Administrator opening in your company. As an MBA with significant global business experience, I have a track record of demonstrated leadership and project management skills. I am a visionary who aligns work with management goals to provide a results-oriented environment. My excellent written and oral communications skills have served to expedite negotiations and helped me interact effectively with associates, project teams, and company management.

I have consistently updated my technology skills and am proficient in web-based applications and computer software programs such as MS Office Suite. I am adept at Internet research.

Please review my resume detailing my education and professional experience to see how my background can benefit your organization. I can be reached at the above address and telephone numbers and would be happy to meet with you and discuss my qualifications further at your convenience.

Sincerely yours,

Devonne Brown
Enclosure

Summary

Applying for a job in today's technological climate need not be intimidating for the mature worker. Create a technology-friendly resume that accentuates the highlights of your career, complete with keywords and simple format. Use action verbs and list accomplishments rather than job duties. State achievements that present your best assets and set you apart from other job seekers. Enlist the help of friends and colleagues in creating employment documents that portray you as a forward-thinking, up-to-date individual.

Think about the concerns employers have about hiring older workers, and then try to dispel many of them by distancing yourself from those stereotypes.

Chapter 3

Using Technology to Find Employment

Technology has dramatically changed the way job seekers conduct their job searches in the last few years. Although local newspapers still run want ads, job seekers who limit their search to this venue miss the majority of openings. Only a small percentage of employers advertise positions in the newspaper. Searching online newspapers increases exposure to the number of want ads job seekers can locate, and decreases the time and money it takes to do it. Dozens of newspapers all across the United States post online, providing 24-hour, 7-day access to job listings and other information. Again, this represents a small percentage of available jobs.

People still walk into companies and drop off resumes or send them by mail, but many places only accept resumes and applications on their websites or online at a company kiosk. Using technology is a must in applying for such positions.

Chapter 2, "Resumes and Employment Letters," addressed the special formatting that is required when posting resumes online. This chapter looks at ways to use technology to find employment through online research and resume and application submission processes.

Make the Internet a part of your job search by investigating everything from a company's background to where the jobs are, to the paperwork required, and the interviewing techniques it takes to get hired. If you do not know how to look for jobs online or how to research companies on the Internet, enlist the help of a friend, relative, teacher, or librarian. Otherwise, you will not be exposed to a majority of the available jobs.

Many companies' websites have a link where you can submit a resume or fill out an online application. It is important to carefully follow the instructions on each website so that your information will be processed. Incomplete information could keep you from being considered for a job.

Researching Companies Online

Where is the demand for your skills and expertise? The quickest way to find this answer is to take advantage of the power of the Internet. Performing online job research enables you to uncover companies that want to hire someone with your talents. Many companies are especially senior-friendly and actively recruit older employees. Targeting these companies will increase chances your resume will be read thoroughly and that you will seriously be considered for a job.

Researching various company websites can lead to information on (1) where the jobs are, (2) which companies need your skills and abilities, (3) which companies target mature workers, (4) company profiles, (5) job leads, (6) job descriptions, and (7) how to apply for available jobs.

How do you find company websites? You can key a specific company's web address into your browser, and be taken to its website. Once there, it is easy to examine the information provided about the company and learn whether it is a suitable prospect. The site may provide a listing of job openings and their description. If you find a job that appeals to you, it may be possible to post your resume and cover letter and fill out an application on the site.

If you do not know the address for a company's website, you can search for the company on any number of websites that accumulate data on companies. These include, but are not limited to job-search-engine.com, wetfeet.com, vault.com, hoovers.com, or similar sites that compile a listing of companies. Another way to search for individual companies is to go to www.google.com, www.yahoo.com, or a similar search engine and key in the name. If the company has a website or other online presence, links for the information will appear. Clicking the link takes you to the company's website. If more than one link appears on a company, it may be worthwhile to scan through the information on several of them to get more detailed background information.

- For example, the site http://www.job-search-engine.com provides a listing of hundreds of jobs at various companies. Log onto the site and click on the word *company* and then click on the name of the company for which you are interested in obtaining employment. You will then see a listing of available jobs for that company, the dates they were posted, the locations, and the job requirements. Sometimes a link to the company's website is listed as well. If you click on the word *category*, you will find a number of available jobs listed by category, such as accounting, administrative and clerical, customer service, etc. A search for jobs by a preferred location brings up a list of states and major cities. Clicking on a keyword displays a list of specialized words such as activities coordinator, animal care, etc.

- Log onto http://www.wetfeet.com for a list of hundreds of companies. Click on the employer button at the top of the screen. An alphabetical listing of companies is displayed. Click on an individual company to get an overview of that company that includes contact information, number of employees, financial status, and more. The site has a link for job seekers and another to a careers and industry section that addresses trends, markets, job openings and their key descriptions. Company searches can be done by keying in a job title or by keying an address or ZIP code. That narrows your search to jobs you would actually want to fill, rather than wasting time searching thousands of unacceptable ones for your situation. The site compiles jobs from various newspapers, websites, and other sources to provide an extensive resource.

- Experts at http://www.about.com provide valuable information on all areas of the job search process. Browse the Explore Our Topics box until you find career planning to access articles on the topic. Click to open the link, and then click the topics in the Must Read section, which include articles on career planning, career training, career change, quizzes, fastest growing jobs, and more. Sign up for a free career newsletter in the appropriate box by providing an email address. You can also search for jobs by ZIP code or type of position.

- At http://www.hoovers.com, click on the companies tab at the top of the page to browse for hundreds of listed companies by name, location, or industry. You can find information on projects, industry trends, company profits, competitors, and company profiles. In addition, the site provides expert advice on starting and operating a business, technology, and other topics. There is also a link to resources.

- At http://www.thingamajob.com, you can sign up for a free account and find information on locating jobs by category or location. Click on *find a job* to browse hundreds of jobs in various industries. Click on the words *career center* to find a variety of articles on job hunting advice and employment resources. You can also post your resume on this site.

- The website http://www.vault.com provides company names and website links, as well as other job search information. You can join in a number of industry blogs, including a new careers blog, and community discussion groups. Search for information on professions, industries, and education. The site also includes career advice, resume writing advice, cover letters, salaries, career change and advancement, and more. Sign up for an account; both free and paid subscriptions are available. You can post a resume and choose whether to let employers view your contact information or keep it private and access only your posted abilities, skills, education, and experience.

You need not know for which company you would like to work. Do a general search by field or industry to find employers. For instance, key in a specific field such as hospital employment, tourism, IT, forestry, etc, to find companies that employ people in those fields. Once you have a company name, you can enter that name into a search engine to find general contact information or a link to its website.

Another way to search for jobs via the Internet is to key in the word employment. This will bring up a listing of general employment sites you can access to learn of possible job openings and also to post your resume for employers to see. (Employment sites are discussed later in this chapter.)

Some specialized career websites offer a wealth of information for all job seekers, which mature workers can use. Check out http://womenforhire.com to access a job board that you can search by keywords and locations. You will also find lots of job search strategies, advice, tools, and seminar information, as well as a listing of career fairs put on by Women for Hire.

The websites listed are examples of what is available on the Internet. Your search may turn up additional resources. Widen your search as much as possible to secure as many prospects as possible. Information on the Internet is in a constant state of change. Therefore, the sites listed in this book are subject to change at a moment's notice. In addition, research with an open mind as not all information provided on the Internet is factual.

Take Charge

Perform a general Internet search to find the websites of several companies in an industry in which you would like to work. Check sites such as http://www. job-search-engine.com and http://www.wetfeet.com and perform a Google search for the word employment or similar term to find companies with which you are unfamiliar.

Research Company Websites

Why should you search a company's website? What information should you obtain? The answers to these questions depend on what you need to know in order to find a job that meets your needs. As previously stated, company websites offer a great deal of information. Some things to look for on a company's website would be answers to the following questions:

- What products and services does the company provide?
- What new product developments are projected?
- What financial information is provided to indicate the company's stability?
- Are there recent newsworthy articles about the company?
- How many employees work for the company?
- How many locations does the company have?
- If the company has multiple locations, is information provided on employee relocation requirements?

- What are the names and titles of top management?
- What positions are available?
- Are positions full time, part time, or temporary?
- Is there advancement in the company?
- What is the salary range?
- How long has the company been in business?
- How is the company organized?
- What are the responsibilities for the open positions?
- Are positions physical in nature?
- Are positions performed indoors/outdoors? Manual labor or mental labor?
- What education and certification is needed for employment?
- What software is used in the company?
- Is knowledge of particular equipment or tools needed for positions?
- Does the company accept resumes and applications online, by mail, or both?
- Does the company have an annual report online?
- What is the company's mission statement?
- What does the company have to offer you?
- What are the operating hours?
- What type of facility does the company have?
- Who are the company's competitors?
- What is the company's culture?

Answers to all of these questions may not be on a company's website, but many of them will be. Anything you can learn about a company in which you are interested will put you in a better position to make the best decisions about whether you would like to work there and help you learn how to apply for a position.

In addition to checking general facts about a company, determine who the key players are in the organization. If you know the names of top management and personnel directors, you can do a Google search to find out their duties within the company, their education and certifications, and whether they have written articles or had articles written about them. This in turn could help you during the application and interview process.

Take Charge

Search the websites of companies you are interested in working for in order to find answers to questions you have about them. If possible, fill out online applications and submit resumes.

Research Employment Websites

A number of employment websites are on the Internet. Some of them offer career information, career assistance, job listings, and a place to submit resumes that prospective employers can access. Submitting resumes on these sites is a good way to get noticed by someone who is hiring. Employers often do Internet searches using key words consisting of the skills and abilities they are looking for in order to find acceptable candidates. Make sure your online presence is sending a clear, professional message to these employers by building a strong resume that highlights the keywords of your industry.

Here is a sampling of online sites that deal with employment and job searches. Keep in mind the list only taps a fraction of available sites and information. Remember too that web addresses change without notice.

- At http://www.careerbuilder.com, you will find information on locating jobs, careers by category, job hunting advice and resources, recently posted jobs, career fair postings, a free salary calculator, and a free career quiz. You can search for jobs in your area by keywords or categories. Post a resume and build an online profile on the site. Career Builder displays jobs and their links. Click on the link to find information on the company, pay scale, type of industry, available employment, job requirements, location, contact information, and more. Sign up to have Career Builder send automatic email updates of recently posted jobs of interest to you.

- Information on low income government programs can be found at http://www.govbenefits.gov. Browse for information by state, category, or agency. A click on the Advocates button at the top of the screen displays links to Community Advocate and Partners. Partners contains links to some federal government departments, and Community Advocate contains guides to various benefits of the federal government. Click on Community Advocate and then click on the link Guide to benefits.gov for Unemployed Individuals to see if you may qualify for job training and placement services. You will find information on the Job Opportunities for Low Income Individuals (JOLI) Program and One-Step Career Centers provided by the Workforce Investment Act (WIA). Click on the link Seniors Guide to benefits.gov to learn if you may qualify for the Senior Community Service Employment Program (SCSEP).

- According to the U.S. Department of Health and Human Services website, the department accounts for nearly a quarter of federal outlay. The site at http://www.hhs.gov lists jobs in the department, how to find and apply for them, pay and benefits, and education and training programs. Type in your own questions in the frequently asked questions box to get quick responses.

- Veterans and their families can find job information on http://www.fedshirevets.gov. The website provides accurate, useful information in one place for those who have served the country. Click on looking for a job, and you will find three sections that provide information: veterans, transitioning service members, and family members. Each section provides information of interest to veterans and their family members, such as job preferences, details on how jobs are filled, and a number of useful links and education/training resources. Click on the agency directory button for a list of offices and available programs specifically for veterans, including contact names and email addresses. The site links to http://www.nationalresourcedirectory.gov, which is a resource for wounded and injured veterans and their families. Click on employment and find information on job services and employment resources, internships and apprenticeships, and transition assistance. A link to employment associations and organizations provides over a dozen links for organizations. Take full advantage of this site if you are a United States veteran.

▪ You can search for government jobs at http://www.usajobs.opm.gov. Go to the site and set up an account (free) and fill in your personal profile. Read the tips for using the federal resume builder. Various federal resume formats are required for different jobs. Read the requirements carefully and then create a resume using the step-by-step guidelines. The site allows you to build several versions of your resume and use them to apply for the jobs listed on the site. You can search for and apply for jobs in cities and states all over the United States. You can also store a request at the site that enables you to receive an alert for job openings that fit your background. Click on the status button to check the status of your application(s).

▪ The site http://www.employmentguide.com lists over 100,000 jobs, and has featured employers; you can browse by states, towns, and ZIP codes; job seekers resources; job searching; work from home jobs; education information, and listings of jobs in specialized areas (healthcare). You can sign up to have job alerts sent to your email address.

▪ On http://www.monster.com, you can post a resume and enter a profile, search for jobs, and use the career tools and advice section to access articles on all areas of finding a job and career development, including career search, company and industry research, networking, and so forth. Use a free salary calculator, take advantage of the advice forum to see what other job seekers are doing, and participate in community discussions on many topics. You can sign up for Monster alerts and save posts of job openings for future action.

▪ Http://www.higheredjobs.com posts jobs in the field of higher education. Search jobs by category, type, location, or specialty area. Sign up for a free account, post a resume, and request job alerts for your city and area of expertise. The site offers career-related resources, news, and articles.

▪ Google has a directory at http://directory.google.com that organizes topics into categories. Click on Business; then search the category employment. You will find links to information on careers, resumes, job search techniques, and more. Click on Job Search for over a thousand links to web pages of sites devoted to employment, such as indeed.com, job-hunting.org, jobsearch.about.com, jobs.net, jobseekersadvice.com, and others. The directory has links to job searches, careers, job fairs, interview advice, and more.

- Http://employmentspot.com lists jobs by city, state, and industry. The website has employment articles, tips, and careers, as well as links for researching companies (for example, vault.com and business.com), job listings by companies, and company listings. In the resources section, find dozens of links to sites for job seekers. For example, the interview link accesses many articles on topics such as proper interview attire, questions interviewers might ask, branding (building a professional online presence that hiring managers and recruiters can find to learn about you), and other career-related information.

- CareerOneStop at http://www.careeronestop.org is sponsored by the U.S. Department of Labor, Employment, and Training Administration. The site provides information on occupations, salaries, career exploration, education, and training. You will find several videos and articles on resumes, letters, applications, interviews, and other such topics. The site also offers links to all state employment offices. State employment sites list a wealth of information and help for the unemployed. For example, the Pennsylvania website found at http://www.paworkstats. state.pa.us provides information on the Bureau of State Employment, the Workforce Investment Area Program, the PA Occupational Outlook Handbook, the State Civil Service Commission, and more.

- For a variety of information and a listing of noncorporate jobs, check http://www.snagajob.com.

In addition to the general employment sites, many niche websites exist for career information and job listings in specialized areas such as http:// www.hoteljobs.com for jobs in the hotel industry, http://www.biospace.com for jobs in the healthcare industry, http://www.teacherjobs.com for teachers, http://www.yourencore.com for scientists and engineers, etc.

Specialized searches for the specific industry in which you want to work may turn up the perfect website for your background. In addition, many colleges and organizations maintain sites for their members and associates.

Take Charge

Check your state website to find out what is offered for job seekers. If your state employment site accepts resumes, post yours. Check to see if the site has a list of jobs you can search. Broaden your search to include other states if you are in a position to move from your home state.

Career Websites for Mature Workers

As a mature worker you can improve your chances of finding a job via an Internet search by narrowing your selections. Not all job websites are appropriate for everyone. Some sites accommodate specific job seekers such as those over 50. Do an Internet search for these sites by typing in "careers for 50+" or "jobs for people over 50" or similar keywords. You will find sites that contain a wealth of information for the mature worker, including specific job openings and how to apply for them.

Take Charge

Search the Internet for websites that link to career-related articles and resources that will help you with your specific concerns and problems. If sites you research accept resumes, post yours. Check to see if the site has a list of jobs you can search.

- Workforce50, formerly the Senior Job Bank, is one such site that caters to older workers. Found at http://www.workforce50.com, the site provides job and career information, preparation, and resources. A job board allows you to do a quick search by state or a more advanced search. The jobs on this site are placed by employers who specifically want to hire mature workers.

- The AARP website at http://www.aarp.org has a work section that offers articles on all areas of the job search process, including writing a resume, where to look for jobs, going from retirement to a job, interview strategies, building a portfolio, and numerous career-related issues. Click on the work section to search for millions of jobs by location, company, or keywords. Learn your rights, find the best employers for workers over 50, and learn what the experts have to say. The Water Cooler section features group discussions where you can contribute and find tips, and the blogs share useful techniques and tips from a wide variety of experts. AARP also puts on job fairs, the details of which are posted on the site.

- Quintessential Careers has information for all job hunters, but there is a section for mature workers at http://www.quintcareers.com/mature_jobseekers.html. This area of the website provides career articles and resources specifically of interest to mature workers. Job seekers can find information on resumes, cover letters, interview strategies, and salary negotiating. There is an extensive listing of job and volunteering sites and resources, complete with accessible links. You can post a resume and search for jobs by type or by ZIP code.

- At http://.www.retirementjobs.com, you will find job resources and advice, a job search guide, career workshops, and a listing of jobs. This site identifies companies most suited to mature workers. You can search by location or type of job, and it is free for job seekers.

- Training for low-income seniors can be found by contacting http://www.experienceworks.org. Check the criteria on the website to see if the training is right for you. They have a government-funded program, Senior Community Service Employment Program (SCSEP), to help low-income, unemployed seniors, 55 and older, get training and job counseling. This program provides workforce transitioning for residents of the states for which they are registered.

Check with the chamber of commerce in your area and surrounding areas to learn more about companies. You can do a search for your local chamber to learn if they have a website and find contact information. Most cities have a chamber of commerce, so if you are planning to move to a new location, you can contact the chamber in that city to get information on employers in that area. Join the chamber for networking support.

Here is a listing of sites geared to workers aged 50+ to get you started. Keep in mind that sites are removed and added continuously.

- http://www.primecb.com
- http://www.aarp.com
- http://www.retirementjobs.com (articles about job searches)
- http://www.workforce50.com
- http://www.jobs4point0.com
- http://www.seniors4hire.org
- http://www.retiredbrains.com
- http://www.retirementlifematters.com
- http://www.snagajob.com
- http://www.50plus.com (Canada)
- http://www.enrge.us (Employment Network for Retired Government Experts)
- http://www.execunet.com (not just 50+)
- http://www.fortyplus.org
- http://www.retireeworkforce.com
- http://www.quintessentialcareers.com (not just 50+)
- http://www.monster.com (Age Issue Message Board)
- http://www.experienceworks.org
- http://www.seniorjobbank.org
- http://www.employmentdigest.net (employment tips and news)
- http://www.jobsearch.about.com
- http://www.indeed.com (not just 50+)
- http://www.scrore.org
- http://www.maturityworks.com (UK)
- http://www.nia.nih.gov/HealthInformation/ResourceDirectory.htm (resource directory for older people from the National Council on Aging)
- http://www.aoa.gov (The Administration on Aging)

Take Charge

Search the Internet for websites of interest to mature workers, post you resume, read articles, join community discussions, and check out the job board.

The benefits of knowing as much as you can about a company include these:

- Helps you find a position suited to your needs
- Gives you an idea of what types of jobs area available and their descriptions
- Gives you information on key personnel
- Gives you information on the hiring process for that company
- Gives you basic facts about the company

The majority of employers accept resumes online through their own websites and other sites where job seekers post their resumes.

The Internet is a good place to network by signing up for discussion forums and groups of interest to you. Ask for advice and share information to establish an online relationship with like-minded people. Communities, discussion boards, and online groups are places where you can go to get information on a particular topic (for example, jobs). One such online gathering place is found at http://www.eons.com/groups/group/careers-for-boomers-and-50- plus.com. Join them to give and share advice about finding a job.

If your skills are rusty, you can often find free training online. Microsoft has tutorials on their MS Office programs. The educational website http://www. internet4classrooms.com has technology tutorials, including MS Office and other software applications. In addition, some universities, temporary agencies, and state career centers offer free online courses.

Social Media

Today's companies use all sorts of social media to get the word out about their products, services, interests, etc. The main forms of social media communication are LinkedIn, Facebook, Twitter, and blogs, although many others exist.

More and more companies are using social media every day. You need to know how to use it, too. This is not the time to say you are too old to use technology or have no use for it. Like it or not, we are totally immersed in technology in all areas of our lives. As discussed in Chapter 2, "Resumes and Employment Letters," many companies use technology to find and hire their employees.

If you are afraid of technology, find a tech-savvy person to sit with you and teach you the basics. You can look to relatives or hire a high school student to tutor you. The point is to show employers that you are up to date and willing to learn whatever the company needs you to learn. As technology evolves, you must evolve with it or risk being obsolete. Once you do, a new world will open for you. Younger workers and prospective job seekers are already well versed on social networking and spend a lot of time using this venue. Do not be left out of the competition.

Millions of people use social media to network. Most professions have multiple networking sites and online community groups that share advice. Chapter 4 discusses the value of networking and how to build a network contact list.

LinkedIn is one of the best sites for job seekers. It is a business-oriented networking site to which millions of professionals belong. Hundreds of industries are represented. You build connections by adding contacts and being introduced to new people through your other contacts in the network. LinkedIn and other social networking sites are great for getting in touch with people you worked with 20, 30, or more years ago. By rebuilding past connections and establishing a sizeable contact list, you can take advantage of a wide range of expertise and perhaps network your way into a job.

LinkedIn has several million members in hundreds of different industries, including Fortune 500 company executives. Making connections with members of this vast network can open the door to a number of opportunities. Many employers use LinkedIn and other social networking sites to find employees, which is another good reason to sign up and complete a professional profile.

If you are not established on LinkedIn, sign up for it today and build your professional profile. Your profile will serve as a resume and establish your presence online. Be thorough when completing your profile, keeping in mind this can become a job search tool for you. It is your chance to show potential employers what you have to offer them. It is also a good opportunity to show you are comfortable using new technology.

Search other profiles to learn where people in your industry are working, and then check to see if the company is on LinkedIn or has a website. Check company profiles to see if they are hiring and what types of positions are available. Are there small businesses to which you could apply? Do you or someone in your network know the hiring manager of any of the companies you have researched?

While researching a company online, if you learn the names of the top people, Google them online to see what they are doing. Are they on LinkedIn or Facebook? Can you connect with them? Do some profile tracking to see how they started out in their company and how they rose to their present positions. Check their LinkedIn profile to see what groups they belong to. Can you join those groups? If so, join and participate in discussions by offering advice. This showcasing of your expertise may bring you to the attention of potential employers who scan the site.

Another business network is found at http://www.ryze.com. You can build professional relationships on this network and take part in discussions.

Facebook is a social networking site that allows you to create a profile page and join groups according to your interests and expertise. You can get leads on job openings from friends or find out what people think about working in particular companies. Share your expertise with Facebook friends. You never know where this type of networking will lead.

Many organizations, businesses, and associations have Facebook pages for promotion and information dissemination purposes. It is a great way to reach out to others, take part in discussions, and share information. Hundreds of thousands of businesses are active on Facebook.

Twitter is a form of social media that allows you to comment in 140 characters. Many career and employment websites and experts send out Twitter messages (Tweets) on a daily basis. Sign up for a free account at http://www.twitter.com and search for people and companies to follow. Enter an appropriate keyword(s) in the search box, such as career, career development, employment, or similar word.

Take Charge

Go to http://www.linkedin.com and join today. It is fast and easy. Build your professional profile, upload a picture, and add a resume. Search for people to connect with and add them to your LinkedIn network. Go to http://www.facebook.com and join today using the easy guidelines. Build your profile. Although Facebook is a social networking site, keep your postings professional if you want employers to gain a favorable impression of you. Find and connect with friends, former classmates, colleagues, and others. Sign up for a Twitter account and search for people and companies to follow. All three sites are free to join and use.

Join In

Check to see if any of the people in your network are on LinkedIn and Facebook. If so, connect with them. A check of member profiles will disclose where people work and what positions they hold. Knowing something about the backgrounds of people you are connected with will aid your networking attempts.

Join online communities in your industry and take an active part in discussions and sharing advice. These communities are made up of groups of people interested in the same things. For instance, if you join a group of job seekers, perhaps through a job board, you can participate in discussions on jobs, careers, interviewing techniques, returning to work after retiring, and other advice that could speed your search. Do a Google search to find appropriate communities for your needs.

Join professional organization websites and take part in discussions to establish a presence. Be a contributor by sharing your expertise. Ask for help with your job search, but do not specifically ask for a job.

Http://www.meetup.com is a place you can go to find groups that share your interests. Find a group by ZIP code and interest and learn and share with the members.

Summary

With the wealth of information on the Internet geared toward mature workers, you should be able to find the guidance you need to prepare for a productive job search. Company websites, employment sites, and mature worker sites offer tips on everything from resumes to cover letters to interview tips to information on individual companies.

If you are uncomfortable using the Internet, the best thing you can do for yourself is ask a friend or colleague for help. Otherwise, you are missing out on a valuable resource. After a few quick lessons, you should be ready to do Internet searches on your own.

Engage in the use of social media as much as possible in order to appear progressive and to increase exposure to employers. At the very least, join LinkedIn, build a professional profile, and upload an updated resume.

CHAPTER 4

NETWORKING

Networking is all about making connections and maintaining relationships. We form these connections for a number of social and professional reasons. Our objectives often intertwine—social contacts help us with our careers, and professional contacts become part of our social circle. As a mature worker, you probably have a fairly extensive network. If so, begin or continue to mutually interact with your contacts and form dependable connections. If you do not have a network, use the tips in this chapter to put together a list of contacts.

Creating a solid support system network is important for job seekers, especially as they age. Networking can provide job leads, opportunities, and much needed support throughout the job search process. Who hasn't heard the expression, "It's who you know"? When it comes to finding a job or maintaining a career, the network of people you know, and people they know, can be a tremendous resource both personally and professionally.

On a personal level, it is tough to go it alone in conducting a job search in a healthy economy and even tougher in a poor one. Add age to the mix, and the search becomes more challenging. Why go it alone when you can solicit help from individuals who are willing to help you stay positive and motivated?

On a professional level, why not utilize the experience, knowledge, and assistance of people who offer it to you?

To make networking effective, be willing to ask for and accept help from people you know. In return, offer your time, knowledge, and assistance to them. This two-way process of helping one another creates an effective network.

When searching for a job, it definitely pays to know people who:

- Will motivate you and help you remain positive.
- Know your qualifications.
- Can help you put together a winning resume.
- Know how to find job openings.
- Know of job openings at their companies and will refer you to their management.
- Can give you information about their companies such as products, services, and types of positions available.
- Know of job openings at their friends' companies.
- Can introduce you to people who do the hiring at their companies.
- Do the hiring.
- Place individuals in jobs (example, temporary agencies and government programs).
- Provide advice.
- Offer to mentor you.
- Can teach you a skill that you need in order to compete in today's market.

What Do You Want?

Before building a contact list, decide what you hope to gain from networking. Do you need information about your industry? Help with a skill or a resume? Job search advice? A reference or referral? A mentor? An introduction to a mutual friend? Motivation or support? All of these things are possible to obtain with the right network.

Searching for a job is not only hard work but also discouraging at times. What can networking do to improve the situation? Networking is a bond with people who can lend a hand when needed, whether for friendly support or professional advice. Close friends and associates you can call on when you have a problem or are feeling low give you the strength to face the difficulty. Your contacts can cheer you on, support you, inspire you, and encourage you. They can rally round when you need a boost of positive energy.

Determining your purpose allows you to tap into the perfect contacts for your specific needs. Personal and professional networks are both important. However, this book concentrates on building a professional network you can draw on for your job search needs, career questions, and professional advancement.

Networking with the right professional people can foster the determination you need to keep going amid disappointing job rejections. Networking makes the job search easier when qualified, competent people are able to impart valuable contact information, tips, job leads, technological expertise, industry information, and so on. Professional networkers often get together to brainstorm ideas and talk strategy—something beneficial that job seekers can apply.

If you already have a job, your network can provide support and insight as you advance in your career.

A viable network can enhance your job search in many ways. Get together with network contacts to:

- Discuss job progress
- Bounce new ideas off one another
- Review one another's resumes and portfolios
- Discuss where the jobs are
- Strategize how to ace the interview
- Ask for referrals
- Ask them to be a reference for you
- Offer to be a reference for them
- Offer your expertise to them

Networking is not all take without any give. Sharing job hunting strategies and information can be equally beneficial to all parties involved. The more you are willing to share about conducting your search and job leads suitable for your network contacts, the more information and leads you may uncover from others. Your contacts can help you create your resume and cover letter, advise you about job opportunities, refer you for openings, introduce you to people who do the interviewing for their companies, and expose you to valuable job search information. You can reverse the roles and make yourself available for your contacts in return.

Once you secure a job, your network contacts can advise and guide you as you advance in the position. Networking is about long-term relationships.

What Job Search Help Do You Need from Your Network?

Think about what kind of help your network contacts could provide that would make your job search easier. Look over the list below to determine in which areas you need the most help. Write down your networking needs.

- Motivation
- Support/encouragement
- Learning a new skill
- Information on the latest industry trends
- Preparing a resume
- Submitting a resume online
- Reviewing a resume
- Interview tips and a mock interview
- Spreading the word about your qualifications
- Advice on how to job search
- Job leads
- Job referrals
- A job reference
- Camaraderie with like-minded people

> **Take Charge**
>
> Make a list of what you hope to gain from your networking contacts. Include personal and professional desires.

Build Your Network

Everyone already networks to some extent through associations with family and friends. This personal support is needed throughout life. Professional support is also needed during the life of your career. Building a professional network expands the circle of people with whom you are associated to include people who can help with your career. The most successful networks include a mix of personal and professional contacts.

To put together your network, consider everyone you know. The obvious ones who come to mind are friends, relatives, and coworkers. How about neighbors and people from your church and community? Do you know the majority of members in clubs and professional associations to which you belong? Can you add teammates from a sport you play or have played in the past? Do you know your local retailers, waitresses, and bank tellers? What about your doctors, dentist, and hairstylist? All of these people are potential network contacts.

Keep adding to your contact list by including former and current classmates, teachers, professors, work associates, and supervisors. Add everyone you can think of, and do not worry about how well you know the person. The objective is to build your network beyond your direct contacts. You will decide later which contacts will make the best connections.

After you have exhausted the supply of people you know, think about people your contacts may know. For instance, list people your family members, relatives, and coworkers know. While compiling the list, you may even recall that you are on friendly terms with these people. One of them may be able to connect you to the right person when you need it.

Now that you have a growing list of contacts, look into other sources to find people and information. Do you know any highly successful people you can model or write to and ask for advice? Can you ask about research in the field they have completed? Can your friends give you the names of people you can approach to find answers to questions about the industry in which you want to work?

As stated in Chapter 3, "Using Technology to Find Employment," company websites provide lots of valuable information. Access company websites and peruse listed personnel to determine if you know anyone. If you do, consider adding them to your network. If you do not know anyone, perhaps another network contact can introduce you at a future meeting or event.

Check social network groups for people you may know. Chapter 3 discussed the benefits of joining LinkedIn, Facebook, and other sites. Do a search for people you have had connections with in the past and those you currently work and network with.

Another good information source is company publications, many of which can be found on company websites today. Read company newsletters and journals to find out who the movers and shakers are and what is happening in the industry. Can you contact the authors of articles of interest to you and set up a meeting to discuss their ideas? Do you have the expertise to contribute an article to the newsletter? Can you co-author one with someone else? Reading company publications affords you the advantage of gaining inside information.

Conventions, trade shows, and job fairs draw people from both sides of the employment picture—prospective employers and job seekers. They afford the chance to find out which companies are hiring, what positions are available, job descriptions, and more. Talk with attendees who may be able to pass along information about the companies represented, and introduce yourself to exhibitors to collect appropriate business cards and drop off resumes.

Schools and colleges offer classes in all types of industries and fields of study. Taking a class or seminar gives you a chance to make friends with classmates who have similar interests. In addition, you gain the added benefit of exposure to alumni associations.

Get into the habit of chatting with people at the bank, post office, and stores you frequent. You never know what casual comment might be a door opener for you. If you do not belong to one, join a professional association and a service or community organization. Add people from these venues and any others to your network.

Look for opportunities to meet new people. Isolating yourself will not advance your job search, and it is unlikely someone will knock on your door and offer you a job. You have to put forth effort to expand your network and gain advantages, even if you do not feel like it or are not an outgoing person. You may not always be successful at trying to add contacts to your network, but more often than not you will meet people from whom you can reap benefits in the future.

Take Charge

How many people do you know? Create a networking list with names, addresses, phone numbers, and email addresses of friends, relatives, current and former classmates, coworkers, teachers, and supervisors. List members of associations to which you belong and people you have met at networking events. Add acquaintances such as your bank teller, postal person, and salespeople at establishments you patronize. If any of these people are on a social networking site, record that information as well and join them online. A simple spreadsheet or a card file can be used to store contact information.

Make It Positive

Make your network a positive one by choosing people who are enthusiastic, outgoing, and upbeat. These people will be able to support your positive outlook, which is important to maintain throughout your job search and career.

Avoid negative people and comments that hinder, rather than help, your search. Negativity has an ugly way of growing and sabotaging your efforts. Do not buy into someone else's misery. Instead, drop toxic people from your networking contact list or have as few dealings with them as possible.

Do your part to build optimism among your contacts by constantly reminding yourself and others that an opportunity can arise at any time. Avoid the "poor me" syndrome, which will drive away your contacts.

People are naturally attracted to optimistic, cheerful individuals. If you cultivate a positive mindset and project that attitude whenever you network, you will attract the type of people you want. Additionally, a positive attitude will give you confidence and optimism, which in turn will increase your enthusiasm and ability to achieve success. By sending out positive vibes, you will become known as a person with whom to associate and consult.

How do you remain positive when you need a job and your efforts to attain one have been fruitless? Positive self-talk and affirmations can help you maintain your attitude and cut down on the stress associated with a job search. Keep reminding yourself that positive beats negative in every way when you are looking for a job. To that end, do something positive such as revise your resume, visit temporary agencies and state career centers, search the Internet, and fill out applications. If you have done all of these things to no avail, you should probably do them again. Oftentimes, it is a numbers game when it comes to getting a job.

Can you form a job alliance with a group of your contacts who are in the same position of having to look for work? You could get together and review one another's resume and employment documents or talk about the latest information you have each heard or read about prospects in different industries. You could do mock interviews where you interview one another and offer positive, helpful critiques. If possible, invite career speakers or people to one of your get-togethers who can give advice on makeovers, hairstyles, dressing for success, interviewing, current resume trends, and industry keywords.

Doing something—anything—is better than sitting at home brooding about job loss or the inability to find work. As difficult as it is, keep going.

Step Out of Your Comfort Zone

We all like to stay within the confines of our comfort zone, surrounding ourselves with the familiar. Many times losing a job or searching for a job requires that we leave that familiarity and push ourselves to a new limit. This is particularly true when the familiar is no longer an option, and there is no return to its comfort.

Take a giant step out of your comfort zone by stretching yourself enough to reach out to people you do not know. The thought of approaching strangers is usually not a pleasant one, but the action will more often than not reap benefits for both parties. Find people you would like to meet and introduce yourself. Ask questions that show you are interested in them. By finding common ground on which to build a quality relationship, you can solidify the contact for a future network relationship.

If you are nervous about meeting people and attending networking events, practice some stress management techniques beforehand such as deep breathing, visualizing a successful interaction with a network contact, exercising, reading, or focusing on your ultimate goal of getting a job or obtaining job search advice. When you attend the event, stand tall, smile, and act confident even if you do not feel it.

If you are shy, force yourself to meet at least one new person a week or go to one meeting a month. Take a friend along to alleviate your nervousness. Maintain eye contact and interest when conversing with people. Stand and sit with confidence. If you do not feel like contributing to a conversation, be the best listener you can be.

When you are meeting people in a professional organization, you already have common interests associated with your industry. That could be the starting point of your conversation. The key is to find shared interests that will lead to a satisfying connection. Encourage discussions by asking questions that require more than a yes or no answer.

Take Charge

Approach someone new today and introduce yourself. See if you can find common ground on which to build a connection.

Cultivate Your Network

A list of network contacts is not much good if it is never utilized. Friends and associates come and go in our lives. To make the connections strong, nurture your contacts by staying in touch with them, by being loyal, and by making a difference in their lives. You do not have to touch base every day or even every week. However, do not wait until you want something to begin networking. Call, email, send cards, extend lunch invitations, and meet up with people on a regular basis, whether it is monthly or a few times a year.

Nurturing relationships takes time and work. It means paying close attention to the other person's interests and genuinely caring about them and what happens to them. When people tell you about themselves, remember the details that are most important about them and to them, but avoid rumors and hearsay that tend to be the result of fabrications or revenge. Malicious comments are never worth remembering, and certainly not worth repeating. During conversations, offer comments, advice, and assistance at the appropriate times.

Track your contacts' successes by reading company publications and local newspapers. When you see them, engage in meaningful conversations to socialize, support them, or impart useful information. Treat this attention to people and trust-building as a top priority investment of time and energy. You never know when one of your contacts can use a hand or lend one to you.

Think of networking as an investment today and throughout life. It takes time to build quality connections by reaching out to people and forming trusting, positive relationships. The best case scenario would be to engage in active networking before you need to call on contacts for help, but it is never too late to begin or resume networking.

Although you should make an effort to remember people's names, a name is easy to forget on occasion. It is embarrassing to be caught off guard and not remember the name of someone we met, especially if we were networking when we met. To avoid creating an uncomfortable situation for other people when you run into them after having not seen them in a while, give your name with your greeting. Say something like, "Hi. I'm Carol. We met at the March meeting." This will also give that person an opportunity to state his or her name in case you have forgotten it.

Because the purpose of networking is to connect, be sure to use the contact information you have recorded to stay in touch with people in your network. Call or email to say hello or invite a contact to lunch. If a networking event or a professional association meeting is coming up, call an appropriate contact and ask him to meet you there or have dinner beforehand. Arrange to meet people at the next industry trade show or job fair. Send a contact an article or two of interest on occasion. If you have read about a contact in the newspaper regarding an appointment or promotion, email or call to congratulate her. Following up after initial contact and periodically thereafter is the best way to develop and maintain connections.

Take Charge

Go through your contact list and send a few friendly emails. Send a note to someone who was mentioned favorably in your local paper. Contact someone from your network and arrange to have lunch and reconnect.

Tell Them About Yourself

How well do people in your network know you on a professional basis? What do they know about your area of expertise and job qualifications? Are they familiar with your skills and personal attributes? If they do not know your talents, how can they refer you when they hear of an opening? How will they know if you can do the job or if you even want it? How can they recommend you to their employers? Obviously, if people do not know if you are qualified for an available opening and willing to interview for it, your name will not come to mind.

The point is not to constantly brag about your abilities or bore people, but merely to get your best points across within 10 or 15 seconds during a normal conversation. Blatant self-promotion rarely works. What does is drawing the other person into a conversation where you can work in your attributes. A great way to let people know what you can do is to offer your assistance to them whenever they need it. Offering your expertise and helping others is part of the networking process that can open doors for you and for them.

For example, if you are a teacher, you might offer to train someone in a software program. You might brainstorm job Internet search ideas with someone who is unfamiliar with online applications. If you are a plumber, you might volunteer your expertise to help at a non-profit agency or assist a low income family. The ideas are limitless.

Another way to present your qualifications is to ask your contacts to look over your resume and other credentials, such as a portfolio, and provide feedback. This approach not only gets you needed help, but also showcases your talents. On the other hand, if you need help creating a resume, consult one of your network contacts who is knowledgeable about resumes and whose opinion you value. You may also want to ask individuals from your network to be a job reference for you if they can vouch for your education, expertise, or work history. Offer to reciprocate by being a reference for them.

When deciding what to tell others in your network about your qualifications, keep in mind the attributes employers are looking for in job candidates. Typically, employers seek out people with knowledge and experience who know how to (1) get along with others, (2) solve problems, (3) use current technology, (4) handle a variety of tasks, (5) communicate effectively, (6) save them time and money, and (7) produce the results they need.

Take Charge

Develop a 15-second pitch you can use while networking. Include current marketable skills and your unique abilities and education. Most people will remember only a few details, so make each word count.

Find Hidden Jobs

Many of today's jobs are not advertised, but are filled by word-of-mouth and referrals. Networking allows you to find hidden jobs—the ones not directly advertised to the public. Your network contacts often know of openings as soon as they become available, and they hear of jobs at companies where their friends work. This provides numerous possibilities for you.

People often refer friends and acquaintances to their employers whenever positions become available. If an employer is pleased with an employee's performance, he or she will value the employee's judgment when it comes to referrals and is likely to hire the recommended friend. Employers often find that current employees are the best source of future employees.

Employers often reward their employees with money or perks for referring someone for a job because referrals provide many benefits for them. These benefits may include saving the time it takes to search for employees and go through numerous resumes and applications, saving advertising costs and employment agency fees, and perhaps maintaining a lower turnover rate among employees. When a friend refers you for a job, it can result in a wining situation for both of you. Therefore, tell everyone in your network that you are looking for a job, the type of position you would like to have, your availability, and your qualifications.

If someone gives you a lead for an opening at his or her company, ask about the company's products and services, general mission, and website address. Does he know the job requirements and why the position is open? Take accurate notes and follow up on every lead and piece of information you are given. Keeping a record of the details will help you stay organized and on target.

Locate hidden jobs by contacting your friends and relatives, former colleagues, coworkers, classmates, and even former employers from companies that you left on good terms. Send these contacts an email or letter or connect with them on one of the social networks if you do not see them on a regular basis.

Did you deal with vendors or suppliers in your previous position(s)? These people are an untapped resource. Can you contact any of them for job leads? They usually deal with several companies and know of openings. If you have provided positive customer service to vendors and suppliers you formerly dealt with, they may be willing to tell you of available positions or offer their name as a reference.

Because most of your contacts will not be able to hire you, do not ask them for a job. Instead, let them know what your employment goal is and how they can help you attain it. For instance, if you would like a job in the hotel industry, prepare a resume targeted for a position in that industry. Call on friends to help with the resume and online applications if necessary. Ask people in the hotel business for advice. Join the professional organization for that industry, and let members know you are looking for a job. If you are taking a class or seminar related to the hotel field, let your instructor and classmates know what type of position you would like. Attend job fairs and travel trade shows to introduce yourself to perspective employers, and distribute resumes. Post resumes on hotel websites and fill out applications.

Volunteer agencies and non-profits are always in need of people, and working for them could provide exposure to individuals, information, and other things that could lead to a job. The position may offer you an opportunity to learn a new software program, operate equipment you have not used before, brush up on a skill, or learn a new skill. In addition, you may meet people at the agency or clients and contacts of the agency who may be able to enhance your job search. Many of these agencies are in the business of helping others. By aiding them, you take a step toward getting assistance in return.

In all cases, without exception, if you meet with success when you are given a lead or assistance during your job search, send the person who provided the information a thank you card or a note. This professional courtesy will go a long way toward nurturing your relationship.

Professional and Alumni Associations

Do you belong to a professional association? If not, consider joining one. Check your local library for a copy of the Directory of Associations or search online for an organization that is appropriate for your needs. Almost every industry or profession has an association(s).

There are literally thousands of clubs and associations, and each has a particular focus. Instead of joining one at random, think about what you have to gain from the membership. That answer will help you determine the best group for you. Choose one that aligns with your goals and has supportive members that meet your needs. For instance, if you are searching for a job, join a professional organization in your field. Although the local bowling league would bring enjoyment, you would probably get more job leads from a group where the members are focused on self-improvement, industry trends, and careers.

Professional associations afford members the opportunity to link up with people in their industry and to reconnect with former coworkers, supervisors, and classmates who may be working in the industry. One of the main purposes of professional associations is to provide a venue for people to make connections. Consider joining a professional association in your industry, your college alumni association, and a community organization to widen your network.

How can a professional organization help you find a job? A lot of professional association members who lose jobs will quickly land new ones because of tips from other group members. As a whole, because association members are employed, they know where the jobs are and the appropriate contact people. As members get to know you and your qualifications, they may even offer to forward a resume for you or suggest that you use their name when contacting a company. Think about the wealth of experience, opportunities, and knowledge various professional association members have and what it would mean to your job search efforts if you could tap into those resources. The prospects would be incredible.

Your college alumni association can be an invaluable resource. Alumni organizations facilitate networking among members, and provide workshops, speakers, career fairs, and general job search guidance. Joining a college alumni association is a good way to gather career information, learn of companies that are hiring, and network yourself into a job. Attend alumni events, read the association's publications, and network with members to get the most out of the organization.

Some large alumni associations have local chapters. Your former college will be able to provide information on an alumni association in your area, where you may be able to connect with former classmates among others.

Become an active member in your alumni association by offering your expertise and building long-term relationships. Learn all you can about other members, such as where they work, how they were promoted, what kind of skills and attributes they have, who they know, their strengths, and so forth. Perhaps you will befriend a member who would be willing to mentor you during your job search.

Most professional associations publish newsletters or journals filled with pertinent industry information and a membership directory of contact information. In addition, professional association websites provide contact information, their mission, cost, benefits, etc.

Some professions require continuing education credits or re-certification (for example, teachers, paramedics) in order to maintain employment. Companies in general often reward employees who obtain continuing education credits and may even pay for them. Professional associations often fill this requirement by having speakers at meetings or mini workshops to keep members up to date and informed. The association then issues the continuing education units according to the participation time involved in the event.

With technology in a constant state of change, a professional organization can apprise you of current technological developments and trends in your industry.

Try to attend meetings as often as possible and volunteer to chair a committee or hold an office. Raising your visibility will expand your networking opportunities as more people get to know you and you are able to showcase your skills. In addition, you will have the satisfaction of improving your community and people's lives.

Various personalities will be connected in a professional association, and it sometimes takes an effort to mesh them. To help maintain a positive atmosphere, avoid "playing games," spreading rumors, and joining cliques. Rather, work together with members for the good of the organization and one another.

Be flexible when it comes to dealing with others and implementing plans. As a mature worker, being flexible will show that you are open to new ideas and situations and are willing to learn new skills—traits you want to get across to a prospective employer.

Learn the association's organization and customs by paying attention to who is in charge, who the problem solvers are, who the difficult people are, whose ideas are implemented, and who has the knowledge.

If you cannot afford to join a professional association in your industry, contact them to see if you can attend a free meeting. Many of them will allow you to attend one or two meetings on a trial basis. If you are currently employed, ask if your company pays association dues.

The many benefits of joining a professional association include these:

- Meeting professionals in your industry
- Providing an opportunity to sharpen rusty communication skills and job search techniques
- Learning about current technological developments
- Learning industry trends
- Receiving newsletters and trade journals
- Reconnecting with friends, coworkers, and other acquaintances
- Raising your visibility
- Providing opportunities to showcase your skills by helping the organization
- Finding support and encouragement
- Sharing your expertise
- Receiving a membership list
- Gaining access to the association's website
- Being exposed to a variety of opportunities and events
- Enhancing self-improvement through webinars, seminars, speakers, and association materials
- Getting referrals
- Finding volunteer opportunities
- Access to trade shows and job fairs

Take Charge

Join a professional organization in your field, your college alumni association, or make other arrangements to meet people and network.

Watch Nonverbal Language

Much of the communicating we do does not involve verbal language. Our gestures, mannerisms, tone of voice, posture, and facial expressions say as much as, if not more than, our words. Although people may interpret nonverbal communications incorrectly, their belief generally overrides the untruth. For example, if someone notices that you bite your fingernails, he or she may think you are a nervous person. That may not be a true assumption, but it may be one that negates a favorable impression of you during an interview or it may cost you a job.

Be aware of the nonverbal clues you are giving off when meeting and mingling with people. Ask a trusted network contact to observe your nonverbal language, advise you of problem areas, and offer suggestions for improvement. Video-taping yourself can sometimes be an eye-opener because you may see yourself quite differently from what others do. In addition, we do things automatically that might put a negative spin on our nonverbal communication.

Avoid a crossed-arms stance, which will make you look standoffish. Be approachable. If you feel awkward with your hands at your sides, hold something in one of them such as a glass or a business card. When you shake hands, shake hands. A limp, fishy handshake is memorable but not favorable. If your hands are moist, dry them on a napkin or tissue before shaking. Use minimal and appropriate hand gestures. Avoid distracting mannerisms such as twirling necklaces and earrings, pulling on ties, clearing your throat, tapping hands and feet, and scratching your head. Do not touch anyone, so as not to create an inappropriate situation.

Posture is especially important for older workers because they want to appear energetic and healthy. Slumped shoulders and slouching give your body an aged appearance. Sit and stand straight with your head held high. Let your confidence show. Keep your distance when talking with individuals so as not to invade their personal space.

Greet people with a sincere smile and welcoming words that will build a positive rapport. Never let a bored or angry expression cross your face while networking. Stifle yawns and sighs. Frowns and pursed lips signal disapproval or distaste. Make eye contact, and avoid the tendency to scan the crowd when conversing with someone.

Keep your focus on the conversation at hand. Show genuine interest by listening attentively and with an open mind. Make the other person you are speaking with feel important by giving your undivided attention when he or she speaks. Take part in discussions, but do not monopolize the conversation. Avoid fidgeting and checking your watch every few minutes.

You will have to get out of your seat or out of the corner of the room and mix with others to present a friendly, relaxed image. You need to leave the safety of the circle of your friends and coworkers at some point to socialize with new people; if you don't, you may appear to associate with only select individuals. You have to put yourself out there to build a beneficial network. However, you do not want to work the room, passing out dozens of business cards without building quality relationships with people. Such behavior could suggest insincerity.

Non-Verbal Communication to Consider

- Make eye contact and focus on the person you are networking with; do not let your eyes scan the room in search of other contacts while you are interacting with someone.
- Use a solid handshake.
- Watch your posture—stand and sit straight.
- Display confidence.
- Smile.
- Dress appropriately.
- Display proper mannerisms and gestures.
- Use an appropriate tone of voice and volume.
- Be energetic and enthusiastic.
- Pay attention.
- Eliminate nervous gestures (chewing nails, biting the bottom lip, tapping feet and fingers, cracking knuckles).
- Use proper hygiene.
- Respect the personal space of others.
- Do not touch others.
- Do not fidget, wring hands, pace, squirm while sitting, or play with hair and jewelry.

Pay attention to your voice level, speaking neither too loudly nor too softly. People will want to be able to hear you without constantly asking you to speak up, but they will not want to be blown over by a booming voice. Adjust your tone to the occasion. Periodically nod in agreement in an effort to alert the speaker you are paying attention and that you understand what is being said.

Use good hygiene and dress professionally for business meetings and events and any time you may come into contact with other professionals. (Additional information on dress is provided in Chapter 5, "Attitude, Energy, and Dressing for Success.")

Do not chew gum, smoke, or overindulge in alcohol during networking events and meals.

To impress possible job contacts and prospective employers, promptly arrive at networking events and meals to show your attention to detail, organization, time management, and punctuality.

Use Social Networking

Have you kept in touch with classmates, former coworkers, and professional association members? If not, it may be time to reconnect on one of the social networking sites. (See Chapter 3 for more information.) After you establish connections with former classmates and associates, spread the word that you are looking for advice about your employment situation.

If you use social networking (Twitter, Facebook, MySpace, and so forth) or if you blog, be aware that employers may do an Internet search of your name to find out as much as possible about you. Therefore, consider anything you post online as writing it on a billboard. What would a prospective employer think about the information you put out on the Internet? Once something is posted and circulated on the Internet, it may be there forever, even if you have erased it. Caution friends and family members about posting something unprofessional about you.

Attend Job Fairs

Job fairs provide an excellent opportunity to hone your networking skills as well as to find employment. Many fairs are free and could have from dozens to hundreds of exhibitors. The purpose of a job fair is to attract individuals who are looking for jobs. Some fairs are specialized for a certain industry or trade (for example, IT, hospitality and tourism, and medical); others are general in nature. Attendees have the opportunity to meet with several exhibitors in one location during a specific time period, which provides an overview of the job market and saves time and transportation costs.

Being in the right frame of mind when you attend the job fair will increase your chances of success. Be positive, friendly, and open to possibilities. When talking with company representatives, avoid complaining about people, problems, other jobs you held, or former bosses. This is your chance to show employers your professional best, and that includes dressing in business attire.

By attending job fairs, especially in your industry, you can collect business cards and applications from prospective employers. Paper clip a business card to each of your resumes and distribute them to the company representatives in attendance. Introduce yourself to as many exhibitors as possible; they may be attending to fill specific available positions.

Talk to other attendees while you are there. You may know of an opening that would be suited to that person, and she may know of something just right for you. In addition, you may make a new connection for your network.

The job fair may be crowded with job seekers, but you only need to present yourself to one employer who needs your qualifications to land a job. Also, the contacts you make can lead to valuable information and future opportunities.

Take Charge

Contact your local employment office, library, chamber of commerce, and colleges to learn of job fairs in your area. Make plans to attend at least one job fair in the next few months.

Networking Meals

Sometimes networking occurs over breakfast, lunch, or dinner. Treat the network meal as a professional experience even when you are meeting a contact socially. This necessitates proper table etiquette, good manners, and appropriate actions and conversation. Going to the dinner prepared to carry on a meaningful conversation will ensure that positive networking will take place along with socializing. You need not have an agenda, but talking about industry trends, careers, and job search techniques will skew the conversation toward your networking needs.

A positive attitude and steering clear of controversial subjects like religion and politics will make for a pleasant encounter. Draw the other person into the conversation by showing an interest in his work. Consider this an opportunity to gather information on companies, job leads, and so forth.

If you want to have your resume or portfolio reviewed, wait until after everyone has eaten before placing them on the table.

A few things to keep in mind during network meals are:

- Consume alcohol in moderation or not at all.
- Do not talk with your mouth full.
- Use proper manners.
- Place your napkin on your lap while eating and next to your plate when finished.
- Know which fork to use.
- Avoid messy, gooey, or crunchy foods.
- Do not slurp or burp.
- Cut one bite of food at a time.
- Do not order the most expensive food on the menu.
- Do not mention food allergies.
- Do not talk about watching your weight.
- Do not eat too quickly or sit and graze.

- Sit up straight.
- Be friendly and conversational.
- Dress appropriately.
- Skip intimate, personal information and gossip.

Organize Your Contacts

Gathering information on your contacts will have little value if you cannot find it when you need it or if it is outdated. Maintain current contact information for people in your network by organizing it in such a way that you will easily find it and use it. An Excel file works well as does a simple address book. The main thing is to use a system that is right for your habits.

In addition to typical contact information such as name, address, phone numbers, and email address, record referrals and the individuals who made them, job advice, when you met the person, noteworthy events, and any other information that adds value to the contact.

It is easy to collect business cards and stuff them in a pocket or purse only to be forgotten until days or weeks later when you pull one out and wonder who the person printed on the card is and why you should care. Have a set place to store the business cards you gather, and make it a habit to file them there as soon as soon as possible. To remember why you collected the card, write pertinent information on the back. Periodically purge cards that have lost their value to you.

Networking Events

Be prepared when you go to a networking event. Research the speakers, topics, or other offerings provided at the event. The more familiar you are with a topic, the more you can draw out key points and make a connection in your mind. Being able to relate what you know to what is presented during a speech or workshop will keep you engaged and improve your listening skills. You will also be able to link new information to your needs.

People are attracted to friendly, cheerful faces. Smile and be positive. To show a genuine attentiveness, remember names. Repeat them when introduced, and try to key the name with something that will trigger your memory the next time you see the face. Take note of names, titles, and other information on name tags when you are introduced to people. If one is provided, wear your name tag on the right side so people will be guided to your name when you shake hands.

Have business cards, resumes, and a pen handy. Give and take business cards judiciously. Dress appropriately, watch your body language, and do not chew gum.

Rehearse your 15-second pitch so you are prepared when someone asks you what you do. If you are unemployed at the time, do not come right out and ask for a job during networking events, rather ask for advice toward your job search. Have some ideas for casual conversation to engage people and focus on them while they are talking. Look for common ground by asking appropriate questions about the other person's interests, expertise, and goals.

Do not interrupt people who are in the middle of a conversation when you join them. Wait for a lull in the discussion. Never monopolize the conversation or people's time. Communication is a two-way process: speaking and listening. Listen for key points, and add something appropriate to the conversation when you have the opportunity. Share information and offer your help if needed. Speak clearly using appropriate word choices and proper grammar.

Networking events can be learning experiences where you can get a free education. Pay attention to topics and learn more about them so you will be able to discuss them at future meetings. Build your industry vocabulary by committing to memory industry terms other people use. Increasing your industry-related vocabulary adds to your expertise and makes you someone others will want to engage in conversation.

If you do not understand terms or topics being discussed by people you are not well acquainted with but feel the terms will be helpful in your job search, look up the word later or else ask a trusted colleague in the industry for an explanation. Refrain from letting everyone know you are unacquainted with key terms or unfamiliar with the topic.

Maintain a positive attitude about your job search. Even though you may be desperate to find a job, never let it show in the conversation. Turn things around and discuss strategies you have used and ask for advice.

If you are eating at the event, use proper table etiquette. Avoid too much alcohol. When a networking event is over, take some time to review what you learned and make notes for future reference.

Many times people form opinions, over generalize, and tune others out when they disagree with what is said. You will become better informed if you suspend judgment when listening to others. You may not agree, but if you listen to the entire point, you will be able to make a proper appraisal of the discussion. With complete information, you will be able to arrive at suitable answers and opinions.

If the person you are conversing with is complaining or using abusive language, find a tactful way to disengage or walk away.

Because we live in a culturally diverse world, be considerate of the customs, mannerisms, and behavior of others.

Reciprocate

Networking is not an opportunity to *use* the people on your contact list, but it is a mutually beneficial connection with them. It is an opportunity for people to work together over a shared goal. Keeping in mind networking is a two-way process, share your expertise, skills, time, and friendship with your contacts. Helping others strengthens your relationships and gives you purpose.

What can you do for people in your network? Can you motivate someone else or lift her out of a negative mood? Do you have resume expertise you can share? Can you connect two of your contacts who could benefit each other? Do you know of a job opening that is unsuitable for you but suitable for a friend? Have you recently interviewed for a job and can pass along tips to others? Can you be a reference for a former colleague or classmate?

If someone introduces you to one of his contacts or recommends you for a job, be prepared to give your 15-second pitch about yourself. Have business cards, an updated resume, and a portfolio prepared and available. Be able to discuss industry trends.

As a common courtesy, thank people for their advice and assistance. Follow up by advising them of the outcome of the situation for which they helped. Send thank-you cards when appropriate.

Take Charge

Pass along industry information. Refer job openings. Introduce people from your network list who share mutual interests. Be a willing resource by sharing your talents and skills.

Networking Sources

Where can you find information on people you would like to add to your networking list?

- The Internet
- Telephone books
- Friends, coworkers, relatives, classmates
- Professors
- Alumni associations
- Chambers of Commerce
- Professional associations
- Job fairs
- Trade shows and conventions
- Company websites
- Employment agencies
- Government agencies and programs
- Retailers and companies you patronize

Business Cards

High quality business cards printed with your name, address, phone number, email address, and title or industry will be a valuable networking tool. Choose a businesslike design and format and avoid cutesy and way out icons, pictures, colors, or printing. MS Office and other software programs make it easy to

Tips for Successful Networking

- Do not limit networking to times when you need something.
- Be friendly and sincere.
- Remember people's names.
- Step outside your comfort zone and meet new people.
- Listen attentively.
- Genuinely care about people.
- Respect others.
- Establish a relationship with contacts.
- Stay in touch; correspond regularly.
- Mingle with people you admire.
- Connect mutual friends to each other.
- Give advice and referrals; be helpful.
- Keep expanding your network.
- Recommend people in your network for jobs.
- Express an interest in others.
- Chat with everyone you meet.
- Use business cards judiciously.
- Be positive and confident.
- Share ideas.
- Join in discussions.
- Do not monopolize the conversation.
- Be aware of nonverbal signals you send.
- Wear a name tag at events.
- Mingle with people other than close friends.
- Shake hands effectively.
- Network everywhere.
- Be loyal to your contacts.
- Follow-up on leads from contacts.
- Join LinkedIn and Plaxo.
- Do not ask improper personal questions (for example, "How much do you make?")
- Do not pester your contacts.
- Do not display nervousness or behave over confidently.
- Continuously add to your network.
- Connect with contacts on a regular basis.

design business cards on a home computer. Try a few difference formats (or have a friend design them). Take some time and design a few styles on your home computer, or have a friend do it for you. Once you have decided on an appropriate design and setup, take your sample to a printer.

Store business cards in a case so they do not become smudged or creased. Never use old outdated cards with pen or pencil corrections. Always carry business cards with you, but be selective when handing out the cards so as not to seem pushy or insincere.

When someone gives you a business card, take a few moments to read the information and make an appropriate comment. At the first out-of-sight opportunity, jot down on the back of the card information that will help you remember why you collected the card.

Take Charge

Purchase professional looking business cards or design and print your own. Avoid fancy fonts and gaudy symbols or pictures. Assemble a professional portfolio that showcases your expertise, skills, and accomplishments.

Summary

Networking is a continuous, lifelong process of engaging with people and learning new things. No matter where you go or who you meet, be aware of contacts and information that can help you in all aspects of life, including your career. Make networking an aspect of your day every day.

Network relationships built on integrity, respect, and professionalism will carry you to a new career and guide you through it. Address people as equals and be sincere. When you share your expertise, be sure your facts are accurate. If you give your word to someone, keep it, no matter how busy you are. Keep confidential information to yourself. Once an agreement or confidence is broken, it is difficult to regain trust.

Networking is a long-term relationship. Find ways to complement each other's personality. Suspend judgment and avoid gossip.

CHAPTER 5

ATTITUDE, ENERGY, AND DRESSING FOR SUCCESS

Good and bad things occur throughout our lives, and there are many things over which we have no control. No one is immune to difficulties. One or two events like being fired or downsized out of a job do not represent our entire life, but they can dominate it in a negative way if we are not careful. Our perception of what happens to us sets the tone for our moods and reactions to events. If we change our perception to see events in a positive way, our attitude will reflect it.

Being out of work or stuck in a dead end job can devastate your self-esteem; however, do not diminish your sense of worth by berating yourself. Most people go through several jobs and multiple careers in a lifetime. You are more than your occupation. You have talents, skills, and experiences unique to you. Believe in yourself enough to know that you are a competent person, and you can conduct a successful job search.

Display a Positive Attitude

Job seekers must convince employers they are a perfect fit for the job. Enthusiasm, sincerity, and a positive outlook can help you have a successful interview and overall job search.

When your attitude choices are optimism and pessimism, why not opt for the positive instead of the negative? What will daily brooding, complaining, and lack of a job accomplish? Why complain about bills and personal problems?

Thousands are in the same situation. Why not strategize a way to solve these problems instead?

Thinking positively does not mean choosing to ignore difficult circumstances in favor of displaying a cheerful attitude to mask your true feelings. It means facing difficulties with a belief that things will improve, and maintaining a bright outlook. Searching for a job in a tough economy, especially as a mature worker, is a challenging situation that demands the stamina a positive attitude can bring. Drawing on an optimistic attitude will enable you to look for opportunities and solutions that will bring about positive change in what seems an otherwise bleak situation.

The success of your job search will depend on your ability to handle even the difficult days with a positive attitude. Where a negative attitude can create a victim mentality, a constructive one can give you a feeling of being in control. Everyone has problems of one kind or another. Having a positive outlook allows people to move forward. The negative feeling of being trapped in problems often brings an emotional downturn and a sense of being overwhelmed. These negative feelings keep a person immobilized, and nothing will be accomplished.

It is difficult to remain positive 24 hours a day, especially when problems bombard you. Although your attitude may be negative at times, try to pull yourself out of the slump as quickly as possible. Every time you have a negative thought, counteract it with a positive one. Even a simple reminder of something good you have in your life can defeat a negative thought. For example, if you keep hitting a brick wall during your job search, remind yourself that you have skills some employer may need, and it is a matter of finding that employer. If an interview falls through, go back to your action plan and take steps to secure another interview or job lead. Perhaps call the interviewer and ask why you did not get the job and if he or she could give you suggestions for future interviews you may have.

Asking an employer why you did not get the job you interviewed for will let you know if there is something different you should do for future interviews. Often, answers you gave during the interview, a mannerism you displayed, a skill you neglected to mention, or similar minor infraction is what cost you a position. Learning this information from the previous interviewer could give you an advantage for future interviews.

You cannot assume you did not get the job because of something you did or said. Someone more qualified or skilled could have been chosen for the position. Brooding about positions you did not get or berating yourself is not productive. Learn what you can from the situation and move on with a determination to find the right fit for you.

If you tend to look on the negative side of things most of the time, you may want to try some of the tips for positive thinking discussed throughout this chapter. Ask yourself how being angry and bitter will help you find another job. Figure out a plan. Finding a positive person to mentor you could be beneficial. Select someone who can review your resume, cover letter, and portfolio as well as help you develop an action plan and practice interview skills. Find someone who will give honest feedback and keep you positive during rejections.

Thinking positively does not automatically make problems disappear, but it can allow you to take a step back and focus on creating an action plan and the steps you can take that might lessen or solve those problems. Instead of anticipating the worst, you assume things will work out, and you take responsibility for moving toward that conclusion as in the previous examples of asking the interviewer specifically why you did not get the job or by asking one of your network contacts to give you an honest evaluation of your job search methods. A positive attitude can spark your imagination and enable you to think of innovative ideas and then give you the determination to carry them through.

Employers look for employees who will fit in and bring positive energy to the workplace. No one wants to hire a complaining, unconstructive pessimist. Negative attitudes spread through a workplace and poison the environment. Before long, the negative individuals run the workplace into the ground. To prevent this scenario, employers seek cheerful individuals who will fit in with other company personnel and be problem solvers, not problem creators. Positive attitudes spread through the workplace just as negative ones do. Conveying positive qualities during the interview will move you ahead of unpleasant or detached job candidates. What can you do to brighten your outlook? See the tips listed in the next section for inspiration.

Tips for Maintaining a Positive Attitude

- Smile; be cheerful and friendly.
- Focus on the best possible outcome.
- Turn challenges into opportunities.
- Avoid using excuses.
- Take personal responsibility.
- Develop positive work habits.
- Visualize a successful outcome.
- Listen to upbeat music.
- Read uplifting stories and books.
- Make new friends; visit with old friends.
- Get involved.
- Do not argue.
- Be kind.
- Take time for yourself.
- Give yourself credit.
- Help someone else.
- Praise someone's efforts.
- Do not criticize yourself or anyone else for a day.
- Know what you want.

Be Flexible

As anyone who has ever worked knows, unanticipated problems happen no matter how much planning is done. Flexible individuals seem to handle these unexpected occurrences with ease, while others fold under the pressure. Flexible people consider various approaches to problems and choose what they feel is a viable option. If that does not work, they change course and find another option. They are not stuck in place with whatever happens to them.

As an older worker, you have your work cut out for you when it comes to convincing an interviewer that you are a flexible thinker. Many employers believe mature workers will not be flexible enough to handle unexpected problems when they arrive. These employers may perceive that older workers are too set in their ways to apply any option other than the one that has always been implemented. How flexible are you? Do you get upset if things do not go as planned? Do you consider multiple resolutions or rely only on the way things have always been done? Do you hate change or do you look at it as an opportunity to grow and reinvent yourself?

One step you can take to increase your flexibility is to break out of your normal routine and try different things. Get up earlier and do something for yourself like exercising, writing, journaling, and so on. Have a full breakfast instead of cereal. Enjoy drinking your coffee on the patio instead of during the drive to work. Explore a different route to the store. Delight in a bath instead of a shower. Take a chance and do something that you have not tried before. Taking risks, even slight ones, will do a lot to ease unfounded fears and eliminate negative self-talk. As you become successful at handling the unexpected, your self-confidence will improve, allowing you to find creative solutions to other problem areas of your life.

It is easy to get discouraged and quit trying to look for opportunities to land a job. Make a point to change your routine and do something different as your job search stretches into months. If you have never done an online job search, go to http://www.monster.com or one of the other employment websites, and scan through the jobs. Submit your resume to an appropriate position on the website. If none are applicable, submit your resume to the employment site so employers can view it. If you have not made phone calls to prospective employers, get out your phone book and look up possible prospects. Take a couple of hours and make telephone calls to gather information and possibly talk to the hiring manager or to set up an interview. Get in your car with a stack of resumes and go in person to companies. If you have an industrial park that has several companies near your home, that is a great place to start. Knock on doors. When you are told a company is not hiring, ask if you can leave a resume to keep on file, and then move on to the next. A rejection is likely due to the poor economic conditions affecting the job market, not you personally.

If you are not ready to make contact with employers, do something else related to your job search. Get a makeover at a department store or have your hairstyle updated. Shop for an interview suit. Invite a friend to your house to go through your wardrobe with you and offer an opinion on what is appropriate for an interview. Be flexible when suggestions are made about changes to your hairstyle, makeup, and wardrobe. The object is to update to a modern image, not hold on to what you have always done.

Persist

Persistence is another trait that will carry you through your job search. You cannot expect an overnight miracle or that a job will appear without any effort on your part. Of course, that may happen, but it is not likely.

It may possibly take weeks or months to find work in a tight job market. Preparing yourself by making a plan and sticking with it throughout the long term can bring success. Many individuals have sent out a hundred or more resumes and applications before landing a job. No, that is not an exaggeration; and yes, their persistence made a difference. If you are not willing to send out a hundred resumes, you are not doing all you can to find a job. What seems like an insurmountable task has been done by other job seekers with whom you are competing.

There is no set limit to how many times you might have to submit resumes and make phone calls, but chances are sending a few will not be enough. In addition, you might have to go on dozens of interviews and second or third interviews before the right opportunity surfaces.

Saying there are no jobs is an exaggeration. Even when the economy is bad, people find jobs. Openings become available because people retire, change jobs, get fired, take extended leaves, and so forth. Temporary positions, another option, become available when companies institute a freeze on new hires and during periods of extra work loads. Challenge yourself to try a new approach, such as taking a position through a temporary agency.

One thing is certain, if you give up the search before finding a position, you will remain unemployed. However, persistence may pay off, and having the right attitude could make a difference in how long you persevere. Prepare yourself to make a hundred employment contacts, not a dozen.

As unemployment continues for months, it may lead to depression and a feeling of worthlessness. Remind yourself that you have many valuable skills and abilities. Better yet, ask someone else to remind you of your attributes. Economies and job markets go up and down all the time. Be ready for the upswing when it comes.

Take Charge

Make a list of at least 50 places you could send your resume. Start sending batches of five to ten resumes at a time.

Assess Your Attitude

Attitude Assessment Questionnaire

What type of attitude do you maintain—negative or positive? Having the right attitude and mind-set will work to your advantage during life and throughout your job search. On the other hand, a negative attitude will keep you from finding success.

Assess your attitude to determine if you are basically positive or negative in your thinking by answering questions such as these:

Do you frequently complain, or are you cheerful?

_____

Is your self-talk negative or positive?

_____

Are you flexible or rigid in your thinking?

_____

Do you wander aimlessly through life, or set goals?

_____

Do you think the worst of people or the best?

_____

Do you expect the worst of situations to happen or the best?

_____

Do you let your health go, or do you keep yourself healthy?

_____

Do you allow circumstances to control you, or do you take control in areas where you can?

_____

Do you go through the day frowning or smiling?

_____

Do you get frustrated easily, or do you go with the flow?

_____

Do you feel useless or purposeful?

_____

Are you dejected or motivated when faced with problems?

_____

Do you accept responsibility for yourself and your actions, or do you blame others for your problems?

_____

Do you flounder along, or do you seek opportunities?

_____

Do you surround yourself with negative people or positive ones?

_____

Do you sit back and wait for things to happen, or do you take action?

_____

Do you have a pessimistic outlook on life, or do you have a positive outlook?

_____

Do you give up easily or persist when things become difficult?

_____

Do you get along with others or not?

_____

Do you stay stuck or work at improving your situation?

_____

Are you a problem creator or a problem solver?

_____

Do you wake up in a bad mood or excited to start the day?

_____

Do you always see the lack in your life, or are you grateful for what you do have?

_____

Answers to these questions should be positive. Your negative answers will pinpoint where you should work on your attitude. You may wish to have a trusted friend evaluate you, too, because it is difficult to be objective when appraising your own attitude. You may not realize you are being negative or see yourself as others or an interviewer would see you.

Of course, it is easier to remain positive when things are going fine, so your answers may change according to circumstances. The ultimate goal is to look for the positives in all circumstances.

Take Charge

Assess your attitude by taking a step back and looking at how you have been approaching your job search and your reaction to the results of that search. Consult with a valued friend and ask her to evaluate your attitude using these questions. Do not take the friend's answers as a personal attack, but rather as a way to help you learn where you need to improve your attitude. Acknowledge negative thinking and behavior, and then take appropriate steps to improve in those areas.

Face Job Search Problems

It is sometimes difficult to maintain a positive attitude during hardships, especially when they take months to abate as unemployment often does. Oftentimes you have to dig deep to find the will to continue or to deal with the problems. Being optimistic and smiling even when you do not feel like it will help turn around your negative mood. Change anger into constructive energy directed at obtaining a job. Imagine how much you can accomplish fueled with such energy.

Call on someone from your network when you feel overwhelmed. You are building a network of support, so use it. There is no shame in asking for help. Someone else may be able to see clearly a step you can take. Oftentimes, the one with the problem overlooks a viable action to take. He or she may be paralyzed by despair or depression. A friend could be a sounding board to provide answers and the balance in thinking that you need to see clearly, to lift the despair, and to push you into taking a step and then another one.

As discussed in Chapter 4, "Networking," build a network of positive people who will benefit and sustain you. Searching for a job is frustrating enough without listening to miserable people complaining about the state of the economy and how difficult it is to get a job. That attitude does nothing to remedy the situation and only serves to drag people further into despair. Surround yourself with positive people who believe they, and you, will find a job and have a better future. Optimistic people are more likely to achieve their goals than negative ones.

How can you improve a not-so-positive attitude when you are searching for a job? Begin by having positive expectations about the outcome of your search. Instead of focusing on the lack of a job, focus on how you can achieve one or perhaps create one of your own through entrepreneurship. Many people look at a layoff as an opportunity to try something they always wanted to do like start a business. If it has been your dream to start your own business, contact the Small Business Administration at http://www.sba.gov for free advice and counseling.

If you are stuck in a rut, move out of your comfort zone any way you can. Implementing new measures may uncover a creative way to tackle your problems. Take some kind of action even if you are not sure what the outcome might be. Inertia leads to listlessness and hopelessness. To break out of a powerless feeling, consider what you can control and what you cannot control. Do something about those things over which you have control and forget about the others, since you cannot do anything about them anyway. One of the things you do have control over is your reaction to circumstances. Do not overreact; do your best to move forward. Believe in yourself and your ability to succeed.

> ## Take Charge
>
> List the things you have control over and those you do not. Let go of the things you cannot control, and find an action to take for those things over which you have control.

Take Steps

There are several actions you can take while searching for a job. You could look over the accomplishments on your resume and savor your successes. If you accomplished something before, you can do it again. You might update your resume and post it online, or contact your local employment office and schedule a meeting with a consultant. You could call a couple of your networking contacts and arrange a brainstorming session. You could conduct online research, or if you do not know how to do it, you can learn from a friend or relative. Do some online social networking on LinkedIn.

Here are some actions you can take while looking for a job and waiting for the economy to improve:

- Take a course; update your skills.
- Work on developing relationships in your network.
- Join LinkedIn, Plaxo, Facebook, Twitter, etc.
- Focus on past successes.

- Deal with mistakes and move on.
- Take some kind of action in your job search efforts.
- Keep up with the latest developments in your field.
- Revise your resume.
- Follow leads and look for more of them.
- Create your own opportunities.
- Sign up with a temporary agency (or additional ones).
- Research companies for which you would like to work.
- Avoid the victim mentality.
- Monitor your thoughts; keep them positive.
- Focus on what you have control over.
- Get sufficient rest.
- Help others.
- Expect the best of people and circumstances.
- Have faith that things will improve.
- Practice stress reduction techniques (discussed later in this chapter).
- Call everyone you know and tell them you are looking for a job.
- Post your resume on several online employment sites.
- Focus on contacting small companies.

Keep trying to do something positive until you achieve the results you want. For instance, if the job lead a friend gave you does not work out, find another one. If you have not heard from employers to which you have sent resumes, send some to other employers. While waiting for an answer to applications you submitted, consider taking a temporary position or volunteering. If need be, change your tactics and consider whether your skills and abilities would transfer to another industry. Research that field. Be realistic about whether you can work again in your former field. Some job losses are irreversible and lost forever. Reevaluate what you want, and change outdated goals that are not working. You may have to lower your expectations of the salary you previously made, the title you had, and the type of position you held.

When your life is going well, be thankful. Focus on the good things you have, including family, friends, a strong network, possessions, and the like. Even in the direst situations, you may be able to find hope or learn something worthwhile that you can apply to other similar situations. Be open to possibilities, and your opportunities will expand.

What do you have to lose by improving your attitude except fear, doubt, complaints, apathy, and inaction? All of these things undermine your confidence and keep you where you are. Remaining upbeat during challenging and demanding situations will benefit you in a number of ways such as these:

- Reduced stress
- Additional opportunities and job leads
- More networking opportunities
- Ability to think clearly
- Ability to attract positive people
- Better health
- Ability to see solutions to problems

Take Charge

Make a list of several positive steps you can take while searching for a job. Take one of the steps today, and continue implementing the steps each day until you reach your goal of obtaining a job.

Self-Talk

We all have endless chatter running through our minds. Some of it is positive, and some is negative. Make a conscious effort to keep your self-talk positive. Avoid telling yourself you are too old to get a job or that no one will hire someone your age. There are plenty of mature people in the workplace. The Bureau of Labor Statistics at http://www.bls.gov gives current statistics on the number of people over 50 who are still in the workforce and predicts the percentage will increase in the future. If those individuals have found employment, you can, too.

Pay attention to what you are saying to yourself and other people all day long. Do you whine and complain? Do you talk about problems and lack? Do you join in negative conversations? Do you berate yourself for being unemployed or underemployed? Do you joke about being unemployed or failing to know how to operate computers? If you answered yes to these questions, your attitude needs improving. By becoming more aware of each negative comment and reactions, you can change them.

Engage in positive conversations with others. When asked how you are, skip the litany of injustices and reply "Great!" Positive words have a cheerful effect on you and others. Most people greet you with pleasant talk and expect the same kind of pleasantries in return. They usually do not want to hear about your problems unless they are close friends or you are meeting them to brainstorm solutions.

Negative words are energy drainers—yours and anyone they touch. When negative talk creeps into your conversations and your mind, counteract it by stating something positive. Anticipate a confident outcome and tell yourself things will work out. Turn to your support network for encouragement whenever you feel discouraged, so they can help you remove doubts and fears.

As an older worker, you may feel age is going against you during the job search. For your part, do not make age a negative issue, and avoid criticizing yourself to the interviewer. Instead, make your age pay off by indicating your accomplishments and the value you can offer an employer. Many times, it is not age but lack of technological skills or current software programs or an updated appearance that keeps mature applicants from being hired. In cases where someone may be discriminating, you will probably not be able to change the other person's opinion of your age. You have the right to contact an age discrimination agency, but your efforts might be futile because discrimination will be difficult to prove. By altering your thinking and approach and updating your skills and appearance, you can allay the interviewer's fear of hiring a mature worker.

Redirecting your thinking from negative to positive can help you feel calm and in control rather than harried. Switching from an out-of-control feeling will allow solutions to present themselves. Keep telling yourself how successful you have been in the past and that you will be successful again. When others give you compliments, internalize them instead of brushing them off.

Practice positive self-talk until it becomes an integral part of your well-being and the way you communicate with yourself and others. If you are having trouble getting started, write out several positive affirmations and repeat them throughout the day so negative thoughts will not have a chance to emerge. Here are some positive affirmations to get you started.

- I am a highly skilled, valuable individual.
- I am determined to find employment.
- I will find a job.
- I have a lot to offer an employer.
- I intend to be employed for several years.
- I have a wonderful support network.
- The economy will improve.
- The job market will improve.
- There is a job for me somewhere.
- I will not overreact to difficult circumstances.
- I will ask for help when I need it.
- I accept that some things are beyond my control.
- I am creating a job search action plan.
- I will succeed.
- I am implementing my job search action plan.
- I am taking steps to find a new job.
- I am energetic.
- I am smart and a problem solver.
- I take daily steps toward my goals.
- I am willing to try something new and creative in my job search.
- I will not paralyze myself with negative thoughts.
- I know what I want and am achieving it.

Take Charge

Go over the list of accomplishments on your resume, and reflect on their value to you and to an employer. Be ready to discuss them during an interview. Make another list of personal things you are proud of accomplishing in your life. Reflect on their value to you.

Be Energetic

Employers look for energetic applicants. Mature workers will have to work harder to convince employers they have the energy and stamina to do the job quickly and efficiently. If you feel you do lack that stamina, know you will have to raise your energy level or risk poor results during your job search. It is not realistic to think an employer will hire you to sit back and rest all day. As employees near retirement, many may feel entitled to take it easy on the job and let others pick up the slack. That attitude will not be helpful when you are looking for work.

Create a receptive climate by setting the right mood for the interview. Walk briskly, stand erect, and shake hands with confidence and a friendly, jovial greeting. Arrive early for the interview, but not too early. During the interview be engaging and upbeat. Smile and be pleasant. Project your enthusiasm through your dress, mannerisms, attitude, voice, posture, and answers. Eliminate nervous gestures as much as possible.

Your effective use of verbal skills can persuade and excite the interviewer by letting her see that you are ready and able to work. Speak clearly and properly. Make your tone lively, but not contrived and overbearing. Use positive words and let your self-confidence show, even if it is waning. Display a calm, relaxed demeanor. Do not divulge too much personal information or ramble on when answering questions. Be confident, but avoid giving the impression you are a know-it-all or have done everything and performed every task imaginable.

Let the interviewer know you are willing to learn and are open to new experiences by citing examples of current software and computer programs you have learned. Tell him about recent education and seminars attended.

Watch for the interviewer's nonverbal feedback to see how he is reacting to your presentation. If you are met with a dull personality, remain cheerful but tone it down a bit. Do not become discouraged if it seems as though the interview is not going well. You have nothing to lose by completing the interview to the best of your ability. You can always count it as a learning experience. Besides, you may be pleasantly surprised by being hired.

If the job seems exciting to you, tell the interviewer. Show the employer you are active in your field and your community by mentioning volunteer work or projects you have completed. Let her know that you plan to work for many years. Revealing what you have learned in researching the company will show your motivation and drive.

After the interview, shake hands with a smile and a thank you. Ask for a business card and when you may expect an answer. Follow up by sending a thank you note or email the next day.

It takes work to maintain an energetic attitude. It can be easier to give up and do nothing than to devise a plan and take action. If you are having a difficult time getting in the right frame of mind, read inspirational material or call on a positive individual from your networking contact list.

One factor in maintaining a high energy level is good health. To sustain a high energy level, keep yourself healthy by:

- Eating properly
- Getting enough sleep
- Drinking plenty of water to keep yourself hydrated
- Exercising
- Losing weight if necessary
- Reducing stress
- Keeping busy doing things you love to do

Manage Your Stress

Stress is caused by a reaction to problems, threatening situations, demands on our time, unpleasant happenings, and similar troubles. These difficulties can occur in all areas of life, including family, finance, health, and work. Even the environment can cause stress with its pollution, noise, and extreme climate conditions.

Everyone experiences stress at one time or another. Stress is a normal part of life. Some stress may even be good for you. For instance, if you have a crucial deadline at work, stress might cause you to operate more efficiently, to avoid procrastination, and to push onward until the deadline. On the other hand, the crucial deadline could cause the kind of stress that leads to illness, an overwhelmed feeling, job burnout, and negative feelings like defeat, anxiety, and anger.

Stress Reducing Tips

To begin to manage stress, take notice of where stress occurs in your life and how you react to various circumstances and events. Then counteract the stress through stress management techniques you would enjoy doing on a regular basis. Check the following list for ideas.

- Write down stressful issues and determine if you have control over any of them. If you can control the issue, take steps to do so. Let go of what you cannot control.
- Walk, jog, do yoga, or other exercise.
- Talk to a trusted network contact; avoid negative people and complainers.
- Work on a hobby, read, or do something you enjoy.
- Meditate or just zone out for a while.
- Do deep breathing exercises.
- Practice time management; plan ahead.
- Clear out the clutter and get organized.
- Eat healthy foods and properly balanced meals; avoid excessive alcohol.
- Listen to your favorite music; sing or dance.
- Spend time with family; play.

- Relax; take a soothing bath.
- Be realistic.
- Take a mind vacation; visualize a special place such as the ocean.
- Make a list of your accomplishments.
- Be grateful for what you have.
- Live in the present moment.
- Get involved spiritually.
- Laugh; watch a funny movie.
- Visit your doctor.
- Learn to accept change.
- Be optimistic.
- Play with a child or a pet.
- Clean the house, the garage, or the yard.
- Get outside and enjoy nature.
- Let go of the need to be perfect.
- Let go of the need to be always right.
- Work on one project or problem at a time.
- Learn from mistakes and move past them.
- Practice being grateful for what you have.

Too much stress causes wear and tear on the body and mind. It can zap your energy, and cause memory problems, mental overload, and nervousness. It can create health problems such as ulcers, high blood pressure, heart attacks, and strokes. Stress can keep you from dealing with problems by incapacitating you, thereby stopping you from arriving at the decisions you need to make. Negative stress is hard to override so that you can function efficiently. If you find yourself incapacitated by stress, you may want to seek professional help.

Instead of feeling overwhelmed and out of control over job loss or your job search activities, learn to manage stress and turn it to your advantage. Challenge yourself to do everything you can to find a job even when you do not feel like doing so. Think outside of the normal job search channels, and do not let fear of the unknown stop you from being creative. Just because you have never posted a resume online does not mean you cannot successfully do it now. Instead of stressing about posting the resume, call a friend to help you do it.

Put your mind to the tasks you need to accomplish and the steps you need to take such as creating a resume, approaching companies, and networking. Learn from what does not work and repeat what does work. A sense of being in control will help lift you out of a hopeless state of mind. Let go of the past, and do not worry and obsess about the future or anticipate disasters that may never happen.

Take Charge

Look over the list of stress reduction techniques and find some that will work for you. Begin including them in your daily or weekly plans. If there are other things not listed that you can do to reduce stress, implement them as well. Change what you are doing occasionally to increase your ability to be flexible.

Get Organized

Organize yourself and manage your time in order to conduct an efficient job search. Make a job-search schedule that fills 10–15 hours a week or more. Consider finding a job to be your current job until you accept a new position. Stick to the schedule you have created even when you do not feel like it.

Schedule your activities on a calendar: updating resume, writing cover letters, adding contacts to network list, arranging network lunches, making employment phone calls, researching companies on the Internet or at the library, scheduling interviews and going on interviews, writing thank you letters, updating your professional image, preparing your interview wardrobe, assembling a portfolio or adding to it, posting resumes online, and creating profiles on social media networks such as LinkedIn.

Carry business cards, a pen, and a notebook or note cards with you at all times during your job search. You never know when you might meet someone who will give you a lead or information you will want to remember. Find a system such a card file, plastic container, or file drawer that works to keep this information organized.

In addition to creating a calendar, keep track of contacts you make, places where you have sent resumes, names of companies you have visited, and the research you have completed. When you are sending a high volume of resumes and applications and contacting multiple employers, you will not be able to remember every detail about them. Keeping a record will refresh your memory if an employer contacts you.

An Excel spreadsheet, a notebook, or index cards work well for keeping information in one place. You can even track the information on your calendar if there is enough space to properly record all pertinent information. Create a system that works for you and that contains the information you will need.

January

Monday	Tuesday	Wednesday	Thursday	Friday	Saturday	Sunday
				1 Update resume	2	3
4 Write several cover letters	5 Network; add contacts	6 Schedule network lunch with a contact	7 Network	8 Make calls to employers	9	10
11 Research companies on Internet	12 Research companies	13 Make phone calls to employers	14 Assemble a portfolio	15 Schedule an interview	16	17
18 Practice interviewing with a friend	19 Prepare interview wardrobe	20 Research company before the interview	21 Go on an interview	22 Send a thank you note	23	24
25	26	27	28	29	30	31

Name and Address	Phone	Email	Method of Contact	Outcome of Contact	Follow Up Made

---

Take Charge

Create a calendar of job search activities. Schedule steps you can take toward obtaining a new job. Decide on a method to keep track of people and companies you contact and information you compile. Put your system into place.

Manage Your Time

Sometimes when you are unemployed and have too much time on your hands, you tend to worry more and accomplish less. Use your time to your advantage to get the right things accomplished for your job search. Write down your goals and the steps you can take to attain them. Prioritize the steps into a daily to-do list, and begin working on them.

When you are planning your resume and letters, making phone calls, and completing other tasks, tune out interruptions. Let people know you are working and cannot be disturbed. Often when people are unemployed, other individuals try to take advantage by drawing the unemployed person into their plans. Learn to say no to requests for your time whenever you have plans to work on your job search. Discourage people from monopolizing your time by making yourself inaccessible. Hang a "do not disturb" sign on your door. Let the answering machine record telephone messages and answer them at your convenience.

Eliminate as many distractions as possible. Turn off the television. Delegate household chores, so you can commit 100 percent to searching for a job. Have a convenient, comfortable place to work or else go to a library.

Set deadlines by using your calendar to schedule job search activities. Tell yourself you must finish your resume by a certain date or that you must visit a certain number of companies or make a specific number of calls by the end of the week. However, be flexible because unexpected situations may occur such as an interview or networking event. Schedule yourself some planning time where you can relax and think of new ideas for your search. Do set reasonable deadlines and give yourself time for breaks so you do not become overwhelmed.

Everyone has a high and low productivity period. Use your high productivity period to your advantage by scheduling your job search tasks during that time. For instance, if you are not a morning person, you might work on easy tasks in the morning such as looking up phone numbers or reading the latest trade journal in your field or a fashion magazine to learn how to dress for the interview. Then, during high productivity periods you could work on your employment letters, post resumes and applications online, and call on employers.

Procrastination can drain you of time. Fear of the unknown and confusion about what to do to find a job can cause procrastination to take hold. Create your action plan for finding a job and write exact steps you can take. Enlist the help of one of your network contacts if you cannot think of steps to take. By breaking down your goal of finding a job, you will have a better idea of what to do and be less fearful of doing it. What is one important step you can take today toward finding a job? Why not do it now?

Time Management Tips

Incorporate these time management tips to make the most of your time.

- Develop a time management system that will work for you.
- Complete a time analysis.
- List job search goals and prioritize them.
- Make a to do list of job search tasks you want to complete that day.
- Do one thing at a time on your list or calendar.
- Use your most productive time to complete difficult and time-consuming tasks.
- Say no to people who want your time when you are working on your job search.
- Do not waste time on job rejections; continue your search.
- Eliminate distractions.
- Eliminate time drainers.
- Do it now; do not procrastinate.
- Set deadlines for yourself.
- Delegate when possible.
- Be on time for interviews.

> **Take Charge**
>
> Do a time analysis to determine how you spend your time. Identify any time drainers and eliminate them. Determine how much time you are devoting to your job search and amend as needed.

Dress the Part

To be taken seriously during your job search, you must dress for the position you hope to attain. You do not have to be a fashion expert, but the way you present yourself gives others clues as to your personality, status, and habits. Think of dressing the part of a job candidate as a facet of your search. Any time you will be in the presence of people who are in a position to help you find a job or hire you, your clothing and demeanor must reflect that of the other individuals in those positions. Otherwise, you risk alienating a possible employer or contact.

If you attend a professional association meeting, volunteer for an organization, attend a job fair, or go to an interview, be sure your professional image implies that you should be considered a serious candidate for a job. The people you come into contact with at these venues may be in a position to hire you or to boost your job search if they like the type of image you project.

Your professional image is the first thing an interviewer notices, and the first impression you make on him cannot be undone. You will be judged by the appropriateness of your clothing and manner, whether seeking a blue collar or white collar job. Send the message through your interview attire and behavior that you are an efficient, self-confident, detail-oriented individual. In the minds of many interviewers, personal appearance is a direct reflection of your work ethic, personal habits, and attitude. Send a favorable message about who you are.

It is a fact that job seekers are judged by the clothes they wear and the professional image they project. Even if you do not believe you should be judged on your attire, the individuals who will be interviewing you have a perception of how candidates should be dressed. If you want to be taken seriously, you must dress in a manner that will command respect and approval. As anyone who is part of a sports team knows, if you want to play for the team, you wear the team uniform. The same goes for business teams, and the suit is the preferred uniform of the business interview. What you wear sends a message to the interviewer and sets the tone for the interview. Send the right message with fashionable, appropriate clothing. Draw attention to your standing as a candidate, not your clothing. You do not want your dress to distract the focus from your skills and abilities.

One of the things you should consider in preparing for an interview is updating your professional image through your dress, hairstyle, and overall appearance. Years of working at the same job or in the same industry may have taken a toll on your image. Job hunting gives you the opportunity to focus on a fresh image for the new position you hope to attain. Presentation is everything during the interview. You may be interviewing with someone quite a few years younger than you are. Give the impression that you are an able job candidate, not an image of the interviewer's mother or grandmother. You want to impress the interviewer with your confidence and sense of style.

Avoid wearing old fashioned, outdated styles if you hope to present yourself as a forward thinking, up-to-date job candidate. The suit you wore to your last interview ten years ago has probably outlived its usefulness in looks and fit. The width of lapels and collars, cuts and leg widths of pants, length of skirts, embellishments, fabrics, and the like can date clothing. If needed, update your wardrobe with a good quality, conservative suit for interviews and outfits appropriate for your first days of work.

For the interview, you will want to dress in an outfit suited to the position you hope to attain or one step above it. If you cannot afford a new suit, perhaps you can find one at a local budget-friendly, secondhand or consignment store or else borrow one that fits properly from a friend. Two organizations that provide free interview clothing are http:///www.dressforsuccess.com for women and http://www.careergear.org for men. Do an online search for other organizations of this type in your area.

Clothing requirements change in the workplace depending on the situation. For instance, interview attire is generally more formal than a typical work wardrobe; and some industries are more formal than others. No matter the situation, though, always maintain a professional appearance throughout your job search in case you come into contact with other business professionals, your networking contacts, and prospective employers. You do not have to live in a suit and tie, but your clothes should be neat, clean, pressed, and presentable when you are in public. If you go to a company merely to pick up an application, dress appropriately, for you may be observed by the office staff who have input on job candidates or you may be asked to interview at that time.

A suit or skirt and pants with a matching jacket are still preferable dress for women, although a fashionable, conservative color matching sweater set in lieu of a jacket will also work. Avoid wearing a dress as it may be too formal or too casual for the interview unless it is a plain, simple style worn with a jacket. Men should wear a suit or pants with coordinated blazer or jacket and a tie. Opt for a conservative, smart look, avoiding trendy styles that come and go quickly. How conservatively you dress will depend on the industry to which you are applying. For instance, legal offices tend to be very conservative, whereas advertising offices are more informal. You may be able to get away with the hunter green blouse under your suit jacket at the advertising office, but forego wearing it in favor of a white silk blouse when interviewing for a paralegal or administrative assistant position.

Interview attire should not be distracting in any way. Stay away from outlandish prints, long skirt slits, plunging necklines, short skirts, tight clothing, whimsical ties, and too casual clothing, such as sweat suits and jeans. Choose the color of your interview attire with care because color sends a message of its own. For example, navy conveys trust and professionalism, and red is bold. Loud, wild colors and prints are out for the interview as are faddish, trendy styles. Navy, black, or gray are the best colors for interview attire, although brown is an acceptable color, and women may choose lighter shades for spring and summer, such as beige or taupe. Solid colors are best, but a pin stripe or subdued pattern may be worn.

Silk or cotton blouses with simple lines in white or pastel colors to match a woman's suit should be worn. Men should wear long-sleeved, white, button-down collared, fitted dress shirts tucked in neatly. Red is a power color, which makes it fine for men's neckties and women's scarves. Subtly colored ties in solids, stripes, or small patterns are professional looking. Ties should be tied properly, and the tip should touch the belt buckle. Choose a black leather belt with a not too large buckle.

Wear clothing appropriate for your age, avoiding clothes meant for someone half your age and clothing that is too small. Outfits from ten years ago will not hold up to today's fashionable styles. Proper fit is essential. Tight or ill-fitting clothing sends a message of personal inefficiency and poor taste. Clothing should also be season appropriate. Your stylish wool or wool blend suit will not do for a June interview. Clingy, velvet, stretch, jersey, or lacy fabrics, sequins and jewels, and party dresses are inappropriate interview and office attire. Baggy and ill-fitted clothing will make you appear older.

Consult a clothing specialist, retail clerk, or a trusted friend for advice on selecting interview outfits and workplace attire. Stick to classics that will endure and buy quality fabrics that will last through many wearings. Several dress for success books can be found in bookstores and perhaps your local library. Watch popular television shows to see what people are wearing and read magazines with fashions for the older population to find clothing appropriate for your shape and size, age, coloring, and personality. Do a Google search of websites and blogs for 50 and older fashion styles. Visit the following websites for ideas:

> http://www.biz.com/apprpriate-business-attire
> http://www.fabulousafter40.com
> http://www.fabover50.com
> http://www.wowowow.com.

Take Charge

Study clothing styles on popular television shows and in suitable fashion magazines to determine what your wardrobe should include. Go through your clothing to determine if it is outdated or modern. Consider giving outdated clothing to charity and building a new, current wardrobe.

Shoes and Accessories

Shoes should be dark, low-heeled, leather dress styles for women and dark, leather business style for men. A woman should wear navy with a navy suit and black with a black suit. Men can wear black for either navy or black suits. Choose a stylish shoe design, not a frumpy one. Sandals, open-toed shoes, and sneakers are not appropriate for an interview. All shoes should be free of scuffs and well polished. Check heels to be sure they are not neglected. Run-down heels and scuffed shoes send a message of carelessness and show a lack of attention to detail. And watch out for the wear that attacks the right side of the right heel of any shoe. It happens because we use that foot for the accelerator in cars. Even after you've polished your shoes, that worn spot will return as you drive to the interview. So give it an extra swipe after you get out of your car.

If dressed in a skirt, women should wear neutral colored hosiery. Men should wear dark socks, never white. Carry a leather briefcase or portfolio and never both a briefcase and a handbag together. For the workplace, women should choose a quality handbag in a coordinating or neutral color and a style that will fit their frame.

Jewelry and accessories should be conservative and modern. Choose silk scarves in conservative colors and prints. Dangling earrings and bangle bracelets, bulky necklaces and belts, facial piercing, multiple earrings, and rings on every finger are distasteful. Small pearl, gold, or silver earrings, simple rings, and conservative watches are appropriate. Men should remove earrings for an interview and wear only a wedding ring and a conservative watch for jewelry.

Belts should be chosen to accentuate your waist; shapeless clothing tends to add pounds. Choose colors and widths that will pull your outfit together. Avoid large, gaudy buckles, cheap embellishments, and worn spots.

Hair and Makeup

You hair and face are focal points. A hairstyle stuck in a decade past will convey that you are not up-to-date. If your look is not modern, you may be conveying that you are not current in your skills either. Hair should be soft and manageable, not dull, flat, frizzy, or over permed. Severe hairstyles will make you seem unapproachable, old-fashioned, and set in your ways. Find an easy-to-care-for cut that you can style yourself between trips to the hairdresser. A stylish cut and the right color can take years off your appearance. If women dye their hair, it should be a natural, flattering color. Choose a hair color or highlights that complement your eyes and skin tone. Dark or gray roots show a lack of attention to detail and neglect. Keep them dyed. Balding men should not wear a comb-over but should seek the advice of a hairstylist.

Facial hair, piercings, and tattoos may create bias or stereotypes. Remove nose, lip, and eyebrow rings and cover tattoos. Neatly trim beards and moustaches. If you have not had your glasses replaced in years, it is probably time to order new frames.

Makeup is recommended to brighten a dull appearance and give a professional look to women. The lack of makeup tends to imply an attitude of not bothering. However, avoid extremes like bright blue eye shadow, clumpy mascara, blood red blush and lip color, shaved fake-looking penciled eyebrows, and heavy foundation that cakes or leaves creases. Use a concealer for dark under eye circles, have unruly eyebrows plucked, and use a moisturizer to keep skin soft and smooth. To brighten dull skin, give yourself a facial at home once or twice a week with steam treatments and moisturizers. In addition, you may want to get a professional facial once a month or every other month. Professional treatments include all sorts of skin treatments and procedures that make your skin look and feel wonderful. Reduce stress, which can also make you look tired and haggard and lead to wrinkles. Also, get plenty of rest to thwart dark circles and drink lots of water for fresh-looking skin.

Proper Interview Attire

Here is a quick recap of proper interview attire for both men and women.

Women's To-Do Dress Tips

- Solid color, navy or gray, conservative suit (skirt or pants) or matching skirt and jacket.
- Coordinated blouse in a conservative color and style (no plunging necklines).
- Skirts should be knee length or longer and have a minimal split.
- Dark colored, low-heeled dress shoes (no open toes or sandals).
- Neutral or light colored hosiery if wearing a skirt.
- Tattoos covered.
- Limited, conservative jewelry.
- Limited make-up.
- Updated, conservative hairstyle.
- Clean, manicured nails (conservative color if polished).
- Portfolio or briefcase.
- Minimal perfume if worn.

Men's To-Do Dress Tips

- Solid color, navy or gray, conservative suit or coordinated jacket and pants.
- Long-sleeved white (or a conservative color) dress shirt in a conservative style and well fitted.
- Tie in a conservative color and print.
- Dark colored dress shoes (no sandals).
- Socks to match the color of the suit (no white socks).
- Tattoos covered.
- Watch and ring only for jewelry.
- Neatly trimmed facial hair.
- Belt.
- Remove earrings.
- Updated, conservative hairstyle.
- Clean, manicured nails.
- Portfolio or briefcase.
- Minimal aftershave if worn.

Use proper hygiene and grooming by showering and using deodorant. Hair and nails should be clean and neatly trimmed. Nail biting can be perceived as a nervous habit, decreasing your chances of being hired for a high-level, stressful position. Women's nail polish should be clear or pale colored and never chipped or smeared. Since you will be smiling at network contacts and interviewers, have necessary dental work done. Consider have yellowed teeth whitened, which will take years off your appearance.

A trip to a department store cosmetic counter or a consultation with a makeup company salesperson can give you an idea of current colors and trends. You may also want to ask for a complementary makeup session and suggestions on products and colors that are right for you. Observe how the cosmetic consultant applies the makeup so you can later imitate the application.

Avoid strong perfume, cologne, and aftershave. The interviewer or other individuals in the workplace may have allergies or may find the scents offensive, which could hurt your chances of being hired.

Take Charge

Make an appointment with a hairstylist to update your hair. Discuss the best color and cut for your type of hair and facial coloring and features. Women should schedule a consultation session at a department store cosmetic counter or a home makeup sales consultant. Add a manicure and pedicure.

Take Charge

Select your interview attire. Be sure it is up-to-date, an appropriate style and color, cleaned and pressed. Try on your outfit before the interview. If possible, get an opinion from a trusted friend. Polish your shoes and make sure they are in good repair.

Casual Business Attire

Once hired, observe the workplace's attire, and then dress accordingly. Casual business attire for most companies does not include blue jeans, T-shirts, sweat suits, flip-flops, and sneakers. Inappropriate pictures and words on T-shirts are generally not tolerated, and hats in an office are rarely permitted.

Casual business attire for men includes business dress or khaki pants, collared shirts, and polo and golf shirts, sweaters, and vests. Casual business attire for women includes dress or khaki pants, skirts, fitted shirts and blouses, sweaters, and sweater sets. Skirts should be to the knee and shirts and blouses should cover the midriff. Shapeless tops, tube tops, spandex pants, and shorts are not appropriate.

Comfortable does not mean sloppy. Clothing should be cleaned and pressed with no tatters, holes, missing buttons, snags, tears, stretched out elastic, or worn areas.

Shoes may be a comfortable, casual style, but no athletic shoes, stilettos, or flip flops. Fashionable flats are available in an array of colors and designs. You will be able to wear classic designs with many outfits. Again, keep shoes clean and in good repair on a daily basis.

Be aware of how color affects your appearance and your mood. Certain colors are best for different skin tones and hair colors. There are four basic color seasons: spring, summer, fall, and winter. Your combination of skin, hair, and eyes will determine your color season. A color consultant can help you select the best colors for your features. Do an online search for fashion color wheels to find more information about how color affects your appearance. Two sites that address fashion colors and other fashion tips are http://www.thechicfasionista.com, and http://www.greatestlook.com/colormatching.html. Fashion magazines project the new colors for each season.

All clothing styles and accessories do not fit all body types. What looks good on a friend may or may not be right for you. Nearly everyone has bought items that turned out to be fashion mistakes. Consult current fashion magazines and books to determine figure flattering styles for your body type. Research online, read fashion magazines, or check fashion books to find more information on styles that are right for your body type.

Purchase clothing you look and feel good in that accentuates your best assets and disguises flaws. Choose attire with the understanding that you will be dressing for work five days a week. Select items for their comfort as well as their appearance. Buy a few appropriate pieces to update your wardrobe. Mixing and matching pieces that go with items you have in your closet will give you the most for your money. Quality fabrics will give you years of wear.

A few basic pieces such as black and navy skirts and pants, coordinating jackets or sweater sets, tailored shirts or blouses, and a leather belt or two can be combined to provide several different looks. Adding scarves, ties, and jewelry multiplies the choices.

Find inexpensive clothing at department store clearance sales, secondhand stores, and online at bargain sites like http://www.overstock.com, http://www.zappos.com, http://www.foreverfashion.com, and dozens of other sites. Do a Google search to find additional sites for clothing, shoes, and accessories.

Take Charge

Go through your closet and make a list of what you need to add to your wardrobe. Look through magazines to determine current styles for older men and women. Check out consignment and secondhand shops and department store sales to add needed items to your wardrobe.

Summary

It is up to you to develop a plan and manage your job search. Once you figure out a plan and the steps you need to take, be persistent in implementing them. Good time management and organization techniques will help you reach your goals.

Use as many job search techniques and contacts as possible. Accept life's ups and downs with a positive attitude. Continuously dwell on a successful outcome.

Maintain a modern professional image throughout your search, and project an enthusiastic, energetic personality. Show that you can adapt to changes.

CHAPTER 6

MISTAKES JOB SEEKERS OVER 50 MAKE

The over-50 job seeker should not rely solely on using decades-old job search techniques and expect to get positive results in today's technological world. Many older people who are looking for work are intimidated by electronic resume and application submissions and are nervous about an economy in which record numbers of people are losing jobs. In addition, they fear age is a stumbling block that they have little control over in this tight job market.

The fear of technology and being intimidated by current job search techniques need to be addressed by the mature job seeker so as not to hurt his chances in searching for and applying for jobs and in conducting an interview. Other negative issues that affect the job hunt are maintaining an old-fashioned attitude and appearance, being inflexible, not tolerating other cultures and generations, lack of enthusiasm, and being overqualified. The mature worker, and every other worker, needs to tackle these issues and to continually grow and change to remain competitive.

Failing to Get Along with Other Generations

Opposites have always had to get along in the workplace—messy workers versus organized ones, outgoing and strong-minded versus introverted, analytical versus social, precise versus flexible, decisive versus spontaneous, and so forth. Now add to this mix the meshing of ages with diverse learning styles, habits, and character traits, and problems and concerns increase among these workers.

Not only are older and younger people working together, but many times their roles have reversed, with younger individuals becoming supervisors of older people. People 50 and over should ask themselves how they will feel about being interviewed by someone their children's or grandchildren's age. They also need to ask themselves how they can come across as a colleague not a parent figure.

After getting a job, people over 50 will have to ask themselves how they will feel working alongside coworkers or being supervised by individuals who are 20, 30, and 40 years younger. Mature workers may very well deal with these situations. They will have to get used to the age difference and not complain about taking orders or working with individuals half their age.

Before you begin your job search, ask yourself how you think you will get along with someone who:

- Is 20, 30, or 40 years your junior
- Is the boss at 20, 30, or 40 years your junior
- Is a Generation X or Y individual assigned to train you
- Is a whiz at the computer
- Is proficient at using email, Facebook, Twitter, and other social media
- Is proficient at IMing and texting
- Embraces any new technologies
- May think he or she knows more than you do
- Regards you as a parent figure
- Has boundless energy and enthusiasm
- Does not let his or her life revolve around the workplace

- Has no qualms about jumping from company to company
- Is dressed casually on a daily basis
- Thinks you are slow and out-dated
- Treats you like you are slow to catch on while training you

Only you know if you can get along in these situations, which are prevalent in a multi-generational environment. Knowing how the majority of individuals in each generation think, act, work, and learn can help you adjust your own attitude and work habits to blend in with those individuals.

Let an interviewer know you value teamwork, cooperation, and fostering relationships with customers, coworkers, and supervisors.

Getting to Know Different Generations in the Workplace

One important strategy for mature workers is to get to know who you will be working with in terms of age groups and how these different groups behave and think. The information provided here is general in nature. There will always be individuals who do not conform to the norms of the group. However, the more you know about other workers, the easier you can adapt to their needs, mannerisms, and approach to work and learning.

Although people of various ages have always worked together, today's companies differ because of having as many as four generations working together. In the past, a few individuals from two or three generations may have worked together, but today it is becoming the norm. Older workers are delaying retirement or re-entering the workforce after retiring. Traditionalists, Boomers, Generation Xers, and Generation Y (also known as Millennials)—four very diverse groups—are working side-by-side in growing numbers.

Traditionalists are those people born between 1927 and 1945. Most are retired, but those who remain in the workplace are often known for their strong work ethic and hard work. The Traditionalists are loyal to their employers, and most have been employed at the same company their entire lives. They are respectful of authority, are used to working long hours, and are team players.

Boomers are those individuals born between 1945 and 1964, representing approximately 77 million people. They tend to be team-oriented, hardworking, respect authority, and view work as personally fulfilling. Their advancement on the job is an important symbol of their accomplishments. They may find technology intimidating.

Generation Xers are those born between 1965 and 1976, representing approximately 59 million people. Generation Xers were on their own a lot while both parents worked or while being raised in a single parent home. Because of this, they are very independent and tend to blur the lines of authority, unafraid of challenging someone who is in charge. Generation Xers are not as loyal to companies as Boomers and often change companies and careers. They are interested in a balance between their work and their lives.

Generation Y, or Millennials, are those born between 1978 and 2000, representing 80 million individuals. They are super comfortable using technology because they grew up with it; therefore, they like to be entertained and stimulated in their work. Millennials are used to playing team sports and like to interact with peers. They like a structured environment where they are told exactly what to do and why they are doing it. They also like feedback on their performance and are respectful.

These various age levels have many unique differences that could have far reaching implications when it comes to training, learning, and working in the same environment. Each generation exhibits behaviors typical for that generation. These behaviors may or may not be the same for different age groups, and, of course, there are exceptions among individuals within each generation. For example, Boomers generally like to work in teams, and Generation Xers prefer working independently. It is easy to see where conflicts might arise when these two groups work together. If you are used to working with project teams and in brainstorming sessions with lots of team feedback and interaction, prepare yourself to deal with younger coworkers who want to do things their way without supervision or assistance in many cases.

Generation Y, or Millennials, grew up with computer technology and the Internet, while most Boomers were well-established before computers hit the workplace. Again, the difference in their level of competency can create a gap. Boomers may feel intimidated, and Millennials may think the Boomers do not know anything. As an older worker, you can assume that your younger counterparts will be computer savvy. Therefore, you must become proficient in the latest software and operating systems if you hope to compete in an environment where computers are prevalent.

Generation Xers were "latchkey kids" who learned to do for themselves while both parents worked, while Generation Y led busy, structured lives with lots of activities and adult supervision. Generation Y has also been more protected because they have lived during violent, volatile times that have seen the Oklahoma City bombing, Columbine shootings, September 11, financial and corporate irresponsibility, home market disasters, and other crises. Therefore, when independent Generation Xers have to interact with Millennials who want to be told what to do and receive feedback along the way, another potentially conflicting situation could arise. As a mature worker, you may be caught in the middle of these two views and have to navigate around them while working.

Training and Learning Among Generations

The learning preferences of the generations varies, which may cause challenges for trainers, mentors, supervisors, and coworkers who train one another. Typically, Boomers are avid learners who like to be in charge of their education, and they are avid readers. Generation X prefers independent study and self-directed projects where they are free to do their own thinking. Generation Y wants specific information on what to do and how they will be evaluated, their attention span is about 20 minutes long, and they like interacting with colleagues. Generation Y also wants lots of feedback and to know what relevance the tasks they are doing have.

Both Generations X and Y like to be entertained while learning; otherwise, they become quickly bored. If Boomers are hired to train Generation X and Y individuals, they will have to adjust a teaching style they have used in the past. If the Boomers are being trained by Generation Xers, they may become frustrated if the Xer expects them to know how to do something after being told once or after having the Xer fix a computer problem without explaining how to do it.

Because all employees will have to be trained or train others on occasion, it is a good idea to make everyone aware of the various learning preferences of different generations; otherwise, an employer risks alienating or losing quality workers. Even a Generation Y employee's need for constant feedback could irritate a Boomer or Generation Xer who is training her. The advent and increased use of technology coupled with varied methods of facilitating learning in students over the years has created unique problems. For example, both Generation Y and X employees are comfortable with computer-based learning, whereas Boomers may prefer an actual trainer. An employer should employ various means of training to accommodate all learners; if she doesn't, generational problems may crop up.

Take Charge

Find a tech-savvy younger person to teach you how to be more proficient on the computer. Pay particular attention to this individual's teaching style. If you have not worked with younger people, consider volunteering for a group or organization where there are a number of them so you can experience how they think and behave.

Interacting in a Multi-Generational Workplace

In order to get along with various generations, learn the work habits and preferences of each generation. Although individual personalities vary, some general assumptions can be made and, therefore, make the workforce compatible and the workplace friendlier. Boomers like to be respected and acknowledged for their accomplishments. They tend to have a good work ethic and like to participate in decision-making and being made to feel a part of the team.

On the other hand, Generation Xers do not put as much stock in authority figures and teams, preferring to work individually without close supervision. They are comfortable with new technology and embrace change. In fact, because they change jobs often, they should be encouraged to take on new responsibilities and learn new skills to keep them with the company. Working hard to advance within the company is not their major objective, and they like to have an active family life.

Generation Y, or Millennials, need a lot of guidance because they are used to participating in activities with adult supervision. They want to be told how they should do the job and what is in it for them if they do it. They expect lots of feedback to be sure they are performing up to standards and making a difference. They are respectful of authority and like to work in teams or with peers. They have a short attention span and are used to instant gratification. Both Boomers and Generation Xers may have trouble adapting to this short attention span.

As a rule, Generation Xers are not impressed by authority figures; they treat everyone the same. They prefer an informal work environment and are tech savvy. They like flexible work hours where they can come and go as long as their work is done. For them, there is more to life than work. For Boomers, work is life. When Boomers encounter this lax attitude, dress, and work view, they may begin to question the Generation Xers work ethic and professionalism. In return, the Generation Xers may feel the Boomers are out of touch and old-fashioned.

One thing an employer can do is encourage Boomers to be mentors so their work ethic is instilled in younger workers. If you are a mature worker interviewing with a Generation Xer, you may want to offer to be a mentor or coach to younger employees, especially Millennials who need the constant feedback. Offer to share your knowledge with younger workers.

If you feel you get along wonderfully working with someone who is decades younger than you, become a beneficial resource for other mature workers who do not get along as well with the younger generations. Offer to give them some tips on the best way to deal with the styles and preferences of various generations.

Unwillingness to Change

The extent to which the mature worker is willing to change often determines her level of success during a job search. As discussed in Chapter 3 "Using Technology to Find Employment," many companies require that job applicants fill out online applications and submit resumes electronically. This process could confuse older workers who are used to mailing resumes and showing up at a company in person. However, anyone unwilling to use this new employment technology will miss opportunities. Likewise, anyone unwilling to consult company websites and complete online research will be at a disadvantage during the job interview.

Think about your answers to the following questions to determine if there is a better way to conduct your job search.

- Where can you find a mentor to help you with your job search?
- Could a Generation Xer give you some pointers or even upload your resume on a company or employment website?
- Could a Generation Xer teach you how to use a software program more efficiently?
- What can you do to keep sharp in the workplace, and who can you get to help you?
- Where can you find a mentor to acclimate you into your new environment?
- Is there a Generation X or Y individual from whom you can model job search techniques?
- Is there someone from a younger generation who will give you feedback about how well you are carrying out your job search and what you could do better?

Take Charge

Find a Generation Xer who would be willing to discuss interviewing with you and tell you what a young interviewer might think of a mature applicant. Ask the Xer if he has any suggestions to help you dispel many of the myths about older workers.

Another challenge mature workers face is the inability to find employment doing what they have done before. As they enter this difficult job market, they may have to forget about replacing a former job with a similar one. Whether losing a job or re-entering the workforce after a few years, the type of work individuals once did and the position held may be gone permanently. This calls for creativity on the part of the job seeker to re-direct skills and expertise.

The skills that had served older workers well for years may not be of use to another company if that company deals with innovative ideas and highly evolved technology. Older workers may even have to move on to a new field if the field in which they were previously employed is no longer a viable option. For instance, manufacturing jobs may not be coming back; a waitress may no longer be able to stand for hours and carry heavy trays; traditional printers and newspapers are going to electronic publishing, eliminating the need for individuals who operate printing equipment, and so on. Those individuals who are willing to adapt and use their skills in other fields often find more opportunities than those who only want to interview for the same type of job they previously held and in the same industry.

Instead of trying to pursue that dead end way of thinking, branch out and consider how your skills can be used in another industry or a totally different type of position from the one you previously held. What are your current skills and in what other fields can you use them? What are your transferable skills that you have learned from all past work and educational experiences? Where can you apply them in a different field? Have you considered training for a new field?

Younger workers are not only open to change but welcome it. A younger interviewer may be concerned that older workers are stuck in their comfort zones and resistant to change. And many older workers are. They must face the fact that past skill and knowledge success does not always equate to future success in the same way for these young interviewers. DOS programming and obsolete software programs an older worker may have used at a former workplace, dated marketing plans, etc., may no longer be wanted by a prospective employer, and younger interviewers may not be able to relate to these outdated skills at all.

Put your past work experience and your prior life experiences to work for you instead of against you. Get creative when letting interviewers know how you arrive at solutions to problems, learn new technology, get along with a wide range of ages in the workplace, and search for a job. Show them specifically how your skills can fit the position you want.

Another issue Boomers might face during an interview and on the job is being given vague job descriptions rather than the clear-cut job descriptions that usually spelled out their duties in the past. Because Generation Xers prefer flexibility, a Generation X supervisor may run the workplace without assigning clearly defined roles to employees, or the supervisor may change an employee's role and duties without notice. This may cause a Boomer to question the wisdom of the supervisor. It could also cause a poor job fit or unrealistic expectations on the part of the employee who questions what needs to be accomplished and who is expected to accomplish it. On the other hand, most Generation Xers appreciate being mentored and may be open to suggestions for how duties should be assigned.

Job descriptions usually indicate that other duties may be assigned, which covers whatever the employer wants an employee to do on the job.

Because it is difficult to make personal changes yourself, enlist the help of a friend to bring success. Do not let an unwillingness to listen to and accept new ideas sabotage your efforts. Being set in your ways will not get you far with most employers.

Take Charge

Make a list of your work skills and transferable skills. Think about how the skills could transfer to another field or type of position. Search out positions where your skills will be needed.

Unwillingness to Be Innovative

As mature workers near retirement, they often coast along and let the younger people come up with the innovative ideas. To remain competitive in the workplace, older workers must use their wide range of experience to bring new ideas to the table. Generation X and Y individuals often want to change things from day one much to the dismay of many Boomers who resist change. However, all generations must come together to produce the best results for the company, and change is inevitable.

During an interview, do not just say you are a problem solver and innovator. Back up your claims by giving specific examples of the creative ways you solved problems and handled specific projects. If you have employed unusual methods for saving money, increasing productivity, or improving workplace procedures, tell the interviewer. Focus on results-oriented accomplishments instead of your combined years of experience that may have no relevance today.

If you want to keep your job or obtain a new one, never stop demonstrating to employers how you are a creative problem solver and innovator in your field. Mention any computer courses you have taken or are taking while looking for employment and any seminars on technology you have attended.

Older workers must often reinvent themselves to fit a position for which they have the skills and abilities to handle but that the interviewer may not recognize. This takes enormous creativity to convey their worth to interviewers and employers and convince them that you are the right person for the job.

Take Charge

Make a list of specific examples of how you have contributed to past employers and increased their profits or productivity. Think of a creative way you solved a problem during a past job.

Overqualified

Listing 50 or 60 accomplishments spanning your 30-year work history could turn off a younger interviewer instead of impressing her. The red flag will go up signaling your age. What may be more important than listing your accomplishments is letting a prospective employer know how your accomplishments can help her company. Focus on specific skills and past duties, not your previous titles, which may make you seem overqualified.

How do you get the positives in your background across to an employer? Limit the years of experience you list on your resume and that you discuss during the interview so as not to turn off the interviewer. Jobs you held decades ago probably have no bearing on the current job for which you are applying. Why bring up decades of experience that is not required for that position? Having too much baggage, even in the form of experience, should not be mentioned. Too much experience may threaten a younger interviewer rather than impress him. Instead, slant your resume and your answers during the interview to the specific job you are interviewing for by tailoring your background to that position. Do not understate your abilities, but do not overstate them either.

When an interviewer says, "Tell me about yourself," he does not want to know what you have done for the last 20 to 30 years or want a 15-minute discussion of your life. He wants to know how your experience and education relate to the position he needs to fill. Highlight a few of your experiences or projects. Brief answers are best, and relating specific examples of how you were successful on a project or in dealing with customers and clients will serve you well. Avoid the "tell me about yourself" trap set for people who like to talk about themselves, especially when they have decades of experience and are trying to impress someone.

During the interview, showcase strengths such as your strong work ethic, energy, flexibility, and up-to-date skills. Can you provide a specific example of a problem you resolved? Can you give an example of a workplace project you worked on and the end result? Can you show how you can resolve conflicts? Can you show that you are energetic?

Convince the interviewer the expertise that comes with your age will benefit her in a big way and that you plan to stay with the company and become
an asset. Let the interviewer know you feel there is always something new
to learn, especially with technology and you are willing to learn it.

If you are looking for a job with less pressure or that will afford you time for
your home life, tell the interviewer that is why you applied for a job that seems
to be for a less qualified person.

Not Embracing Technology

As technology takes over the workplace and the world, knowledge and facts
are easy to acquire when the need arises. Therefore, many professionals in
their fields need to find a way other than through their expert knowledge to
appeal to employers. One such way is through technological skill development.

You may feel you are computer savvy because you have been using a company software program for years or a Windows operating system. If these
programs are not the latest being used, they are going to be essentially worthless to an employer who is up to date. You may be a quick learner, but many
employers are not willing to give you the time to learn the new program while
on their payroll because they have ample candidates to choose from who do
have the software and program skills they need.

Be truthful about the value of your skills to an employer. If you have been out
of the workplace for a number of years, you will have to get training on the
latest technology. You will need basic computer literacy because most jobs
require some computer operations. Everyone must continually update technological skills because technology is constantly changing. Employers are looking for the best fit for their organization with regard to technological
competency.

Employers today need employees who are proficient in a variety of software
programs, especially Windows-based software including Excel, Word, and
PowerPoint. Being able to use the Internet to research is important.
Employers need employees with the ability to email efficiently, and not just
check email messages. They should be able to send emails with attachments,

forward messages, copy and paste sections from one document to another, and use email distribution lists. Employees should be familiar with Outlook, an electronic calendar, and similar programs, as well as fax and copy machines.

Workers who are afraid of technology must come to terms with learning how to use it if they are to be competitive in this job market. It may be worth noting that software, computers, printers, and all things technological become obsolete after about six months. There's always something new on the horizon. A subscription to a magazine like *PC World* or something similar can help you stay up with the current trends. Even if you've never used SAP software or a droid phone, for instance, it's better to be able to speak knowledgeably and enthusiastically if these things come up in an interview. A knowing alert look is better than a blank stare. Just to say, "no, I've never used Skype, but I've read about it and I'd love to try it" sends a much better message than to say, "Skype? What's that?" Knowing the difference between Windows and Unix-based open source programs is good too. It isn't just proficiency that employers are looking for; they also appreciate some enthusiasm about new technology. If you're scared of technology, you should get informed and unscared right away.

Take Charge

If you are not up to date on the latest software that employers are requiring in their want ads and job descriptions, make plans to get adequate training.

Lack of Confidence and Low Self-Esteem

When mature workers lose a job and have to look for another one, they are often surprised to learn the extent to which technology has taken over the employment process. Those who are intimidated by technology will find it difficult to find and apply for jobs. This inability to continue their job search pummels their self-esteem.

Being forced to compete with a younger generation that grew up with computers further erodes confidence. When mature workers lack the latest technological skills, they are passed over by employers who find plenty of individuals who possess the skills for which they are looking. After a while, older workers begin to doubt themselves and blame age discrimination.

What is really keeping you from attaining a job? Is it lack of technological know-how? Look at where you need to improve and practice, take a course, or find someone to teach you how to use a computer and the latest software. These skills are not optional if you want to be employable today. Everyone from a sales clerk to a mechanic to a teacher to an office worker to an accountant uses a computer.

Once you have the appropriate skills and technological know-how, tell yourself that you will be able to compete with younger workers and get the job. To raise your esteem even more, look into companies that welcome mature workers. Chapter 3 provides websites to search for these companies, and Chapter 7 gives additional information.

Raising your self-esteem will increase your self-confidence. Some ways to increase self-esteem include:

- Face your challenges head-on to decrease fear and intimidation.
- Take action on your challenges.
- Work on increasing your skills.
- Become proficient at using technology.
- Focus on your strengths when applying for a job.
- Focus on your achievements and how they can help an employer.
- Do something productive every day.
- Walk confidently and smile at everyone.
- Find a mentor or someone to model.
- Eliminate negative self-talk.
- Eliminate self-criticism.
- Everyone makes mistakes; learn from yours.

- Learn from past failures and move on.

- Reduce stress.

- Reward yourself for successes.

- Maintain a positive attitude.

- Read positive, motivational materials.

- Build positive relationships with others.

- Remind yourself that the job market will improve.

Many older workers say they do not understand the younger generation and never will. Reading about the younger generation and actively seeking to work and volunteer with them can raise older workers' self-confidence by easing fears and stereotypes. They can confidently let an interviewer know of their dealings with and understanding of generational issues.

Even just listening to some of the current music, staying informed about what's trendy, knowing who the celebrities and entertainers are who appeal to younger people helps you avoid the fuddy duddy label. Turn off the Motown, and turn on the rap. At least for a little while. Try not to be shocked by the language and behavior of other age groups.

Take Charge

Think about areas of your job search where you lack confidence. What can you do to increase your confidence and raise your self-esteem? Can you call on a friend or mentor to help you? Write down several ideas and begin to implement them.

Taking a class or working for a temporary agency or nonprofit organization can help you improve your skills or learn new ones, which will boost self-confidence when you have to answer tough interview questions about technology or if you must take an employment test using the latest software program.

One thing that lowers self-confidence is not letting go of mistakes. Do not keep reliving past mistakes and failures until you despair about your situation. Think about what you have learned from the situation and how it can help you do better in the future. Everyone makes mistakes, but it is what people take away from the situation that determines whether they are using the challenge to their advantage or their destruction.

Being Unprepared for the Interview

Workers who have held the same job for a decade or more may be at a disadvantage when it comes to interviewing because so many things have changed over the years. If you have not interviewed in years, your interview skills are probably not up to par. Presenting the right professional image is crucial. Remember, the interviewer will often make up his or her mind about a person within the first few minutes. Dressing for success was discussed in Chapter 5, "Attitude, Energy, and Dressing for Success." In addition to proper image, depicting an enthusiastic, energetic persona is essential to give the interviewer the right impression about what you can bring to the company.

Ten, twenty, or thirty years ago, an interviewee could get away with knowing very little about a company. Today's interviewers take for granted that interviewees will have done their homework and researched the company. There is no excuse for not knowing what products and services a company offers and basic information about the employer, the company's locations, and job requirements for available positions. You may even want to check LinkedIn to see if the person you will be interviewing with is listed and what information is available. Read industry newsletters and blogs so you can discuss the latest trends and know the in-demand skills.

A mature interviewee can count on being asked questions regarding technology, especially computers. Using an old operating system or program will not impress employers. In fact, if you do not know the difference between Twitter and LinkedIn, you will be perceived as outdated. Many skills used in today's newly created positions evolved when the jobs were implemented. If a mature employee was never in such a role, he or she probably never learned the newest skills or even heard of them. Therefore, anything you do to update your skills will be looked upon as a willingness to learn whatever is necessary to do the job. Technology is in a constant state of change, so you will have to continually upgrade your computer skills to remain competitive.

If you have not yet upgraded your skills, you may want to look into doing so while job hunting. Waiting and expressing a willingness to learn new software on the job may not be enough to satisfy an employer. Of course, you do want to get across the point that you are adaptable and open to learning new skills, but the more you know going in to the interview, the better.

Many mature workers do not know how to link the skills and experience they have to an employer's needs. Find out what you can about the position for which you are applying and see what similar tasks you have performed in the past. Have you worked on any special projects lately that called on your marketing, organizational, time management, computer, PR, and other skills? Have you attended recent conferences or seminars? Emphasis should be placed on variety and timeliness.

Do not give the impression that you know more than the interviewer and can teach him a thing or two. Confidence is one thing; being an overbearing know-it-all is another. Interviewers do not want to be put in their place. Interviewers who are younger than job candidates will usually not be impressed by experience that is years old. They want to find a candidate who will be a good fit in the organization right now and who is willing to listen to others' ideas.

Practice your answers to typical interview questions such as "tell me about yourself," "what can you bring to my company," "what software can you operate," "what are your current certifications," and "why should I hire you." Be prepared to discuss the latest technology and developments in your industry and use the current terminology in your field. Ask yourself how you can get your point across clearly and concisely and in a way that will sway the interview in your direction. The more you practice, the easier your answers will flow. However, you do not want to over prepare so as to come across as arrogant.

Common Interview Questions

- Tell me about yourself.
- What can you do for my company?
- Why do you want to work for this company?
- What are your greatest strengths? Weaknesses?
- Why should I hire you?
- Give an example of how you dealt with a negative situation in the workplace.
- What was the salary on your last job?

- How well do you work under pressure?
- What pay and benefits do you expect?
- Why are you unemployed?
- What do you know about this company?
- How have you saved past employers money or time?
- How have you increased your productivity?
- Give an example of how you have creatively solved a problem.
- How do you feel about working for a younger supervisor?
- What can you do for this company that other candidates cannot?
- Why have you been out of work for so long?
- What have you been doing for the months you have been out of work?
- What were your most significant accomplishments?
- How long do you intend to stay with this company?

Take Charge

Find a trusted confidant with whom to practice interviewing. Look and act the part of an interviewee and have the friend critique your efforts. Give your answers to typical interview questions, and then discuss the answers with your practice partner to determine if there is any way you can improve.

Never complain about a previous employer or company or about an employer where you were laid off and received a bad deal. Do not show any anger about being fired. Keep the explanation of your job loss brief and neutral.

Do not bring up personal information about your health, finances, and personal problems. Sounding desperate is a turnoff. Never mention that you are ready to retire soon.

Be flexible. If your ideal job or the one you loved going to for years is no longer available to you, your options may be limited to part-time, temporary, projects, consulting, working as a contractor without benefits or insurance, or a lower paying full-time position. Any of these means can lead to a full-time job, benefits, and raises.

If you want to appear progressive, create an online presence through social media, a website, or a blog. All of these avenues are easy to set up. You can also turn your expertise to writing articles for online and print journals.

Wait until you are offered a figure before discussing salary. The interviewer should bring up salary and benefits, not the interviewee. Once a figure is given, you have the option of negotiating. Keep in mind many others may be willing to settle for the offered salary; your negotiations may price you out of range.

Talk about the abilities you have that are relevant in today's market and that set you apart from other candidates in a positive way. Look over your resume prior to the interview and be ready to discuss anything on it. Ask intelligent questions about the position, responsibilities, and the employer's expectations, but do not ask too many questions or talk too much.

When you are called for an interview, make sure you interview for that particular position. Do not give the impression you are looking for just any job right now. State why you want this particular job and make a strong case for why you should be hired. Link your previous experience to the position in a way that makes you a perfect fit.

Create a portfolio that includes your resume, references, letters of recommendations, awards, certifications, and examples of projects you completed. Carry the portfolio with you to interviews and show it to the interviewer at an appropriate opportunity when the interviewer asks about your experience or credentials. You may wish to carry your portfolio in a briefcase. Women should not carry both a briefcase and a purse.

Interview Tips for 50 and Older Job Seekers

- Update your interview outfit.
- Update your hair style.
- Practice interviewing with a 30-something friend or relative.
- Practice your answers to standard interview questions.
- Link your experience to the position for which you are applying.
- Research companies for which you are interviewing.

- Maintain a positive attitude.
- Update technical skills as needed.
- Research current salaries for positions to which you are applying.
- Read about multi-generational issues in the workplace.
- Prepare examples of how you have solved problems, saved an employer money, or increased your productivity.
- Be friendly and energetic.
- Watch non-verbal communication.
- Speak confidently; do not talk too much.
- Prepare and take a portfolio to the interview.
- Limit discussion of your experience to the position for which you are applying.
- Do not exhibit nervous gestures such as playing with hair or tie, twisting earrings or necklaces, tapping fingers or feet, etc.
- Ask for the job.
- Ask when you can expect to hear about the position.
- Relate your skills to those required of the position.

Take Charge

Create a portfolio that showcases your experience and credentials. Limit the material to the particular job for which you are interviewing so as not to overwhelm the interviewer with decades of examples. If you have current certifications, have taken a recent computer course, or have attended a technology workshop or conference, include documentation.

Too High Salary Expectations

You may believe an employer is lucky to get you and your long history of experience, but the employer may believe you come with too high a price tag. Besides, in this era where there are many more highly skilled experts looking for work than there are jobs for them, your competition may know more and be willing to settle for less money than you are.

Employees who have been in the workforce for decades often have unreasonable salary expectations. Face the fact that you may have to take a considerably lower salary than you have been making. Many high-paying jobs have been eliminated and have been replaced with ones that pay a third or half as much. Keep in mind that many younger workers are willing to accept that pay and work their way up in the company.

A difficult part of the interview is likely to be salary negotiations. Check one of the online salary sites so you have an idea of what certain jobs are paying in your area. Find information at http://www.salary.com or http://www.payscale.com, or Google the word salary to find sites that will give you the information you need. Talk to people who are still working in your field, and ask career counselors and temporary agency employees to determine the going salary rates for a position you are seeking.

Once you have determined salaries for your area and the type of job you are seeking, you will be in a position to negotiate any salary offered to you. However, expecting to be paid what you think your experience is worth may not coincide with what an employer is willing to pay you. Many employers are forgoing raises and even cutting paychecks and benefits in this economy.

If you are willing to accept a lower salary, be sure to get that across to the interviewer. Be aware that many people today are also willing to take a pay cut in return for a job. If you are in a low paying job to begin with, know that there are lots of people who are willing to work for or below your wages. Reassess your salary expectations and what you think you are worth.

Errors on Employment Documents

If you have not updated your resume in years, be sure to check out current resume styles and create a new, modern resume. Use concise, value-driven statements, a list of current skills and software, and quantitative accomplishments. Use an attractive style that looks professional, is easy to read, and contains keywords used by employers. Chapter 2, "Resumes and Employment Letters," discusses writing resumes in detail.

A majority of resumes contain typographical errors or misrepresentations of some kind. There is no excuse for having errors on this very important document. Even one error shows you do not pay attention to detail. Proofread your resume carefully a couple of times to avoid typos and poor grammar. Be sure your contact information is complete and correct. Do not rely on spell check; it does not catch all errors.

A resume is important enough to pay an editor or English teacher to edit for you. One trick for editing a very important document is to read it backwards. You are more likely to catch missing words, wrong words, or misspelled words. When you read the same sentence over and over, your brain tends to supply the correct word, even if it's wrong in the document—you literally can read it over and over and not catch a simple typo.

Cover letters should be well written and error-free whether they are sent via mail or email. Never write anything negative, especially about a former employer. Chapter 2, "Resumes and Employment Letters," provides tips for writing cover letters. Follow up job interviews by writing a thank you letter, note, or email.

Give complete and accurate information when filling out applications. Did you include area codes with telephone numbers? Did you give house numbers, correct streets, and ZIP codes in addresses? Is your social security number correct? Did you provide an answer on every line, writing "n/a" if a particular question is not applicable to you? After filling out the application, re-read it to be sure it is error-free. Print or write neatly and avoid messy corrections. Be careful when giving reasons for leaving a previous position. Remain as positive as possible throughout.

Any time you are asked to fill out employment documents, double check your work for completeness and accuracy before submitting.

Lack of Enthusiasm

Many individuals interview for positions they would like to have and feel they did a good job of getting across their good points and their desire for the job, only to be rejected by an employer who feels the candidate did not seem enthusiastic toward the position. You must convey your enthusiasm and eagerness to fill a position through your mannerisms and your words. Tell the employer how you feel about the position.

Display the vitality necessary for getting the job done. This is your chance to erase the stereotype of having a low energy level that weighs on so many older workers. If you do not feel and act energetic, you will be unable to convince an employer to hire you. Why would the employer choose someone for a position if he did not feel the applicant could handle the work?

The position you interview for is important to the interviewer. Never give the impression it is beneath you but you need a job and will take it if offered. You are the one who must convince the interviewer to hire you.

Sit up and listen carefully when the interviewer is speaking. Lean in slightly while answering questions. Let your personality show in a positive way.

Unable to Work with Diverse Groups

Workplaces today are global. That means everyone must learn to accept and get along with individuals from every background and culture. The inability to accept diversity in the workplace will hurt your chances of attaining a position. Never mention anything derogatory about another race, culture, religion, ethnic group, and so forth.

If diversity is mentioned during the interview, let the interviewer know if you have worked with diverse groups in the past. If you have not, mention your willingness to work in such an environment.

Unable to Make a Connection Between Your Background and What the Employer Needs

Sometimes it is difficult for an individual who has been in a position for a long time to make the connection between her skills and what an employer needs.

In a tight job market, where competition is robust, it is not enough to be competitive. You must be better than most candidates, and you must be able to convey that to an employer in order to secure one of the sought after positions.

Explain why you want to work for that particular organization, and give a good reason. Thousands of people need jobs, so simply saying that you need the job will not do. Check the company's website and link what you learn about the company and the position to your reason for wanting to work for the company.

Use figures and examples to show why you are the best candidate to fill the position. Express your interest in becoming part of the team.

Summary

Any job seeker can make a mistake while searching for a job, but the older job seeker should be especially vigilant to guard against the mistakes discussed throughout this chapter. You do not want to give the interviewer any reason to disqualify you for a position. Many times older job seekers feel their age is being held against them when, in fact, they are committing interview mistakes.

An interview is too important to take a chance on being satisfactory. Today's job candidates must stand out among the hundreds of others. Prepare for the interviewer's questions, know something about the company and the industry as a whole, prove yourself through examples, dress the part, ask intelligent questions, and show your enthusiasm. Remember, people are still getting jobs even in this poor economy. Make the employer believe you are one of those people who should get the job.

Chapter 7

Who's Hiring?

Even in a tight job market, there are jobs to be had, and people over 50 are getting jobs.

Of course, jobs exist in low skill, low pay areas, but they also exist in high skill, high pay areas. Getting a high skill, high paying job may take time, education, and employing new job search techniques. The good news is that a number of companies hire and recruit workers over the age of 50. Although it may be more difficult or take longer for someone over 50 to find a position, especially in this economy, jobs do exist, and mature workers are getting hired.

Job applicants over the age of 50 may be surprised to find that they have a variety of career choices they may never have previously considered. According to the U.S. Bureau of Labor Statistics at www.bls.gov, the number of people over 50 in the work force is growing. The Bureau of Labor Statistics *Occupational Outlook Handbook* lists current information on jobs alphabetically by type of industry. You can access this information by clicking on the industry and then on the area in which you would like to work. The *Handbook* also gives salaries, employment projections, the fastest growing occupations, and workplace trends such as productivity levels, employment by age level, number of layoffs, and more.

Chapter 3 of this book, "Using Technology to Find Employment," gives information on the AARP website, where you can browse the list of employers who are likely to hire people over 50. Members of AARP receive the *AARP Magazine*, which provides a wealth of information on careers, employers, finance, and various issues of importance to older people.

As discussed throughout this book, there is an abundance of support and information for people over 50 who are looking to find work, update their skills, or begin new careers. If you are 50-plus and looking for a job, why struggle alone? Use the information provided in previous chapters to research websites, agencies, and other venues to find the assistance you need.

Consider your lifestyle, health, education, financial circumstances, and interests when you are looking for a job, so that you will be more apt to secure a rewarding position where you will be happy. Take into consideration whether you want to adjust your work schedule and how you want to do it. Then ask yourself why you want to work.

- Do you want to find a full- or part-time job, flex time, a work-at-home opportunity, a long- or short-term project, or a temporary position?
- Do you need to work to generate income for daily living expenses, or can you afford to accept a part-time position?
- Are you bored or do you miss interacting with other people in a work environment?
- Do you want a position that will allow you to give back to your community?
- Do you want to work for yourself?

Answers to these questions will lead you toward the industry and type of position most suited to your needs.

Research Job Growth

When deciding where to look for your next job, research the *Occupational Outlook Handbook* to determine where the job growth is predicted to be in the next few years. In that way, you can prepare yourself and update skills for an industry where you will be able to find a suitable job that will be around for a while.

It is best to consult the *Handbook* if you are thinking about changing careers or retraining. If you know where the growth is, you can gear your training to a position in one of those industries. Is there something you always wanted to do or a field in which you wanted to work? Now might be the perfect time to pursue something you have always wanted to try but have been holding off because of a current job or other responsibilities.

Consider how a job in a new industry will fit in with your lifestyle. For instance, is the work physical or mental? Will you have to put in long hours on the job? Can you build on the skills you already have, or do you have to start with some new basics? Is the work something you will enjoy doing? If a job does not fit your lifestyle and interests, it will not be satisfying. Sometimes a complete change of venue affords the most rewarding opportunities.

While you can certainly land a job without furthering your education, you may want to branch out, transferring your skills to other fields or acquiring new ones. Even if you do not retrain or go back to school, never stop learning through reading, networking, and attending workshops and association meetings in your field. Show employers you are willing to adapt to change.

The *Occupational Outlook Handbook* and many websites (some of which were listed in Chapter 3) list senior-friendly jobs and the companies that embrace mature workers. A sampling of these senior-friendly industries includes health care, finance, social services, the government, and higher education institutions, to name a few. It makes sense to apply to a company that values your age and the expertise that comes with it. After researching various sources to find and select individual companies that are appropriate for you, check websites of the individual companies you selected for more detailed information on their available openings.

> **Take Charge**
>
> Consult the U.S. Bureau of Labor Statistics *Occupational Outlook Handbook* to determine the growth industry projections for the next several years. If any of these industries interest you, determine how your abilities and knowledge could transfer to one of these growing fields or learn what skills you would have to acquire in order to obtain a position.

Managing and Directing

Mature workers who have expertise, education, and specialized backgrounds may find positions in an industry that needs their talents. Health care, finance, customer service, and environmental fields offer positions for managers and directors in an endless array of areas. If you have a background in auditing and taxes, customer service, telemarketing, IT, sales accounts, accounting, communications, data analysis, public relations, web design, operations analysis, health care programs, nursing homes, or physical therapy, put your skills to work in management in an industry closely aligned to the one in which you have been employed.

Directors are also needed to coach, consult with, and manage other sales managers. Career coaching and consulting are discussed in the following sections. Align your background and skills to an area of interest for another individual or company.

Career Coaching

If you are an expert in your particular field, you may want to become a career coach and impart your expertise to others. Coaches guide their clients and help them come to decisions that benefit them personally or benefit their businesses. A successful coach can be a sounding board to help clients solve problems and improve the bottom line for their clients' companies.

Career coaches can become certified in their area of expertise. Conduct research on the Internet to find programs and requirements for coaching programs that fit your needs and to learn more about becoming a coach.

Consulting

Consultants advise companies about growing their business, financial information, pricing and cost reduction, hiring and staffing, and a host of other details involved in running a successful business. Anyone with industry expertise and education can become a consultant if he desires. Consultants can make more money per hour than they did at full-time jobs, but they may not get as many hours of work.

Consider offering your expertise and skills to a company on a consulting basis. Some individuals become consultants to their former employers. Many companies hire consultants to work on projects or special assignments. Older workers are perfect for this type of arrangement, especially if they want flexibility and a lighter schedule.

If you are a problem solver who can quickly arrive at solutions and positive results, sell that skill to companies where you would like to consult. Talk up the results you have achieved and how that experience can help the company.

Although consulting is usually part-time work, once you establish yourself, you may be able to land a long-term assignment or obtain referrals to other companies that can use your expertise. If you need full-time work, you can hire yourself out to several different companies as a consultant, and work as many hours as you need.

You can form your own consulting firm and work on a project-by-project basis with several clients. If you establish your own consulting firm, you could employ other consultants and arrange assignments for them.

Becoming a consultant takes planning and dedication, as well as a high energy level, networking skills, the ability to market yourself, record keeping, and good communication skills. You must be disciplined enough to manage your time well in order to complete projects for customers, meet deadlines, and market your services to new clients.

Income is uncertain and often unreliable for consultants. If you do not have clients and the work they provide, you will have no income. Therefore, marketing will be a big part of your consulting business. Keep excellent time records because you are being paid by the hours you put in for a company.

Having a large network of contacts will make it easier to build and maintain your consulting business. Being computer savvy will be an invaluable skill for producing brochures and flyers, creating customer correspondence, and keeping records and a calendar. Sales and marketing abilities will contribute to a steady source of income-producing projects and clients.

Areas of consulting include, but are not limited to these:

- IT
- Health care
- Marketing
- Advertising
- Human resources
- Sales
- Medical practices
- Environmental and energy
- Education

Take Charge

Make a list of your skills and abilities that would be invaluable if you were to become a consultant. Make another list of the companies you would be able to work with as a consultant. Check your networking contacts to see if any of them can direct you to companies who need your consulting expertise.

Entrepreneurship

Millions of people start their own businesses. Retirement or a layoff may create the perfect opportunity for someone who has always wanted to try her hand at entrepreneurship. If you have a particular niche skill or expertise, you may want to launch a business of your own where you can utilize that background.

Before beginning such an endeavor, research your idea. You may want to conduct a survey to see if there is a viable market for your product or service. If there is a market, consider surveying people who might become future customers to learn how to focus your efforts to meet their needs and yours.

Many new businesses fail within the first few years. Create a comprehensive plan for your business to enhance your chance of success. The Small Business Administration (SBA) at http://www.sba.gov offers assistance to individuals who want to start a small business or to those who need guidance with an established business. The SBA website has the following information and more:

- Financial, including loan options and guarantees, interest rates and repayment rules, eligibility requirements, how to qualify and apply for an SBA loan guarantee.
- How to plan your business, including outlines and a small business planner.
- A variety of online training courses and webinars.
- Contact information, including local resources.
- Detailed explanations about how to plan and run a small business.
- Frequently asked questions and answers.
- Articles on a variety of business-related topics.

Another organization that provides guidance on planning and running a small business is SCORE, a non-profit association composed of willing volunteers who will answer your questions either online or in person.

Find information and SCORE office locations at http://www.score.org. The website offers thousands of tips and resources for anyone starting or running a small business. SCORE is a Small Business Administration resource. SCORE provides the following:

- Mentors who offer free, confidential advice
- Online workshops and Webinars
- A newsletter
- Marketing tips

- Business planning advice

- An online small business community

- Accessibility to thousands of volunteers at hundreds of chapters nationwide

- Dozens of business-related online articles

- Information on handling business finances

- Information on preparing and completing business records

- Business tips

- Information on hiring employees

- Information on managing your business

- Frequently asked questions and answers

Owning your own business can provide a nice income while allowing you to pursue your dreams and goals, many of which may have been on hold for years as you earned a living in a full-time job. However, the business may require an outlay of capital and years of operation before turning a profit. Soliciting investors for your business is an option to putting up the cash yourself.

Before jumping into entrepreneurship, create a detailed business plan such as those provided on the Small Business Administration or SCORE websites. If other people are going to be involved in your venture, solicit their opinions and advice regarding the business planning and operation.

If you do not want to go into business by yourself, you may want to take on one or more partners. If you do not want to start your own business, you may want to join one that a friend or former colleague has already started if it meets your needs and you are qualified for a position in the business. You could also look into one of the many franchises and existing businesses for sale.

Take Charge

If you have ever wanted to own your own business, take time to visit the SBA and SCORE websites to learn about available help. Create a detailed business plan. If you do not want to start your own business but can join a friend or colleague in his business, check into the possibility of a suitable position.

Adjunct or Full-Time Teacher or Tutor

Teaching is a wonderful opportunity for the older worker to convey his or her expertise and knowledge to younger generations. Many colleges and institutions of higher education welcome seasoned veterans as instructors. Although many of these jobs are adjunct (part-time) teaching positions, you could sign up to work for two or three different colleges if you want to accumulate additional hours.

Schools hire instructors based on their education and their areas of expertise. Be sure to convey every skill set you have and all areas of expertise in order to have the broadest opportunity. In addition to colleges, the public school system and private elementary and high schools and post-secondary institutions hire experts as teachers on a full-time, part-time, or substitute basis. Teachers' aides are hired on a full- or part-time basis and as substitutes in many schools. A position as an aide usually requires less training and little or no certification.

You will need the proper certification to work in a public school, but many schools will guide you in attaining this certification because there is a shortage of teachers in many fields. If you already have a bachelor's or master's degree in a related field (for example, math, science, or English), you may be able to obtain teaching credentials in a short period of time. A call to a local college can give you the requirements needed to become a certified teacher in your area of expertise or an area that you will enjoy. You might also find information online on your state's website.

Some private schools are not as strict about attaining teaching certifications as long as you are considered an expert in your particular field or industry. Each individual school will provide its teaching requirements. If the school has a website, you may be able to find those requirements online.

Tutoring jobs are available for individuals who have a background in subjects in which students need academic help. Elementary schools, high schools, and colleges use tutors for student's homework and remedial work and in teaching adults basic education courses. In addition, you could do private tutoring out of your home. Many parents hire tutors to help their children with homework.

In addition to educational and certification requirements, many jobs where individuals will be working with children require background checks. Forms and information can be obtained from the school to which you are applying.

If you are not sure whether teaching is for you but would like to try it, consider volunteering as a tutor, aide, or substitute teacher at a youth program, an after-school program, a church, or a school.

Companies and organizations also hire teachers and trainers to work in their company training programs and to conduct individual workshops and seminars. Experts in specialized fields are hired to write instructional materials for any number of specialty areas where employees need improvement and instruction, such as software programs, computer operations, letter writing, telemarketing, and customer service.

Non-Profit Organizations

Work that has a meaningful impact on people, the community, or the country, can be found in the non-profit sector. Although non-profits may not pay as much as other sectors in many cases, the jobs can be rewarding, especially if you like helping people or supporting a charity or cause. There are non-profit organizations, large and small, for numerous causes. If there is a particular cause that interests you, research available organizations in your area and the types of positions within those organizations that may suit your abilities.

Non-profit organizations need a variety of workers in sales, finance, human resources, public relations, administrative assistance, and management just like any other company, and they appreciate the expertise of older workers. There is a likelihood your skills could transfer to one of those positions. Non-profits range in size from the small local office of a few employees to a large organization with a national headquarters and several offices.

If you have been unemployed for several months, volunteering at a non-profit could keep your skills from getting rusty and add to your experience and knowledge. SCORE, one such volunteer program explained more thoroughly elsewhere in this chapter, has thousands of volunteers who provide business information. Use your expertise at SCORE or another non-profit organization to help people. By increasing your visibility through volunteering, you may attract the attention of an employer within that organization or another one.

Small Businesses

Millions of small businesses hire millions of people. Older workers may have a better chance of finding a job at a small business rather than a corporation or large organization. Smaller businesses are generally more willing to give people a chance and many are growing in their industries, which could provide opportunities for advancement and salary increases. A corporate background and years of experience are welcome at small businesses that need the expertise but may not be able to afford to pay what corporations and large companies can.

Small businesses can be an excellent place to develop new skills or sharpen current ones. Lots of small businesses offer specialized merchandise and services, and your experience may complement the specialty. Research various businesses to find a niche suited to your background and your needs.

Use your networking contacts for the best results in finding a position in a small business because they often hire referrals from their employees. Your local Chamber of Commerce or Small Business Administration may have a listing of the small businesses in your area. Once you learn of the small businesses in your area, check their individual websites for information on available job openings and requirements.

Did your company deal with small businesses (for example, printing companies, PR and marketing firms, vendors, etc.)? Make a list of all those businesses you dealt with and the people who were your contacts at them. If you provided the individuals at these companies with excellent customer service, they may be inclined to help you. Contact them to inquire about job opportunities in their companies or ask them for recommendations or referrals.

Applying for a job at a small business often gives you the opportunity to speak face-to-face with the person doing the hiring and learn the specifics about positions. Small business owners are more accessible than individuals who are in large HR departments or who are the CEOs of corporations.

Take Charge

Consult your local phone book and Chamber of Commerce to determine what small businesses are in your area where you might be interested in obtaining employment. Explore those company websites to determine if there are openings and the requirements for filling the positions. If interested, apply for a position or post a resume on the company's website.

Government

A lot of employment opportunities exist in the government, and mature workers are welcome to apply to these positions. Local, state, and federal government offices require a variety of skills and expertise. Think outside the box when considering government employment by applying for a position in Homeland Security, the IRS, the Social Security Administration, U.S. and state transportation departments, parks and recreation facilities, the forest service, veterans' agencies, state hospitals, local and state tax offices, and the like.

A listing of current government jobs can be found on local and state websites. Federal government jobs can be found at http://www.usajobs.gov, the federal government's employment information site. You will need to create a federal government resume following the guidelines on the USAJobs website to apply for a federal job. Only resumes formatted according to the federal guidelines will be accepted. Once you locate a suitable position on the site, post the resume you created and follow the steps to apply for a job.

Health and retirement benefits of the government make jobs inviting even when the pay is not as high as comparable private sector jobs.

You may also want to take the Civil Service Test because many government jobs require applicants to pass the test to be considered for employment. Check your state's website for times, locations near you, and study guides. Taking the Civil Service Test will give you more job opportunities for positions posted on the USAJobs site and elsewhere.

If a political career interests you, start getting involved in local politics, such as city council meetings, and work your way up to higher levels. You may want to begin as an aide or volunteer for a local representative or other official to learn the ropes and to keep current on policies and procedures even though many of these jobs are contingent upon wining an election.

Take Charge

Consult your local phone book for local government offices and agencies where you might be interested in obtaining employment. Explore state and local government websites and USAJobs to determine if there are openings and the requirements for filling the positions. If interested, apply for a position or post a resume on the website.

Health Care

The health care industry is one of the fastest growing fields, and projections are that the trend will continue as the population ages. The industry is also facing a shortage of trained applicants, which means openings will need to be filled. Many different types of positions are available—home companions, medical assistants, lab workers, technicians, pharmacists, pharmacy assistants, physical and occupational therapists, clinical researchers, dentists, doctors, registered nurses, anesthesiologists, physician assistants, hospital administrators, and many others.

In addition to direct patient care, the health care field offers behind-the-scene jobs in accounting, administration, administrative assistants, customer service, medical coding and billing, medical transcription, and others. Positions are available that require little physical demands, which makes them appealing to older workers. Jobs such as transcription and billing can often be done in your home.

Training for health care positions can range from minimal to extensive and may require certification, depending on the position you prefer. For instance, medical transcription and billing/coding training may be completed in as little as six months. Contact your local community college, vocational-technical school, or private trade school for information about programs.

Individuals who would like to be home health care companions should contact a home health care organization to determine the necessary training for companions, visiting nurses, and other positions.

If you feel you have the personality to work in the health care field, you may want to check into the requirements of a position that interests you.

Customer Service

Friendly, accommodating, a good listener—these are skills that make excellent customer service representatives. Older workers make good customer service representatives, because they generally understand what it takes to satisfy the customer, and they are willing to go the extra mile to provide exceptional service to them.

Just about every business needs customer service specialists to provide help and guidance to customers and clients and to solve problems and generate goodwill for the business. If you have a knack for working directly with the public, patience, a knowledge of products and services, and empathy, you may be suited for a customer service position. In addition to these character traits, you will need excellent communication skills, including telephone, oral, and written. A pleasant personality and professional appearance will lend credibility to your image.

Retail

Although retail jobs are not noted for high pay, there are lots of opportunities in sales, and many establishments offer a discount on their products and services to employees. If you enjoy being around people and like to advise them on purchases, retail sales may be the field for you.

Try one of the specialized areas in which you have an interest. For instance, if you have an interest in cars, try an auto parts store or wholesaler. If you are interested in hair and makeup, try a store that sells beauty supplies and products or makeup. Do you like to read? A bookstore or library might be a good fit. Are you a sports enthusiast? Look for a job in a sporting goods store, a stadium, or sports arena.

Many older workers like the flexibility retail affords, such as casual or part-time positions, accommodating hours, and light physical demands. For the individual who prefers advancement and challenges, retail offers management training and positions.

Financial

Positions in finance are attractive for mature workers who have a background or degree in a specialized financial area. Positions in finance include accountants, investment counselors, bank branch managers, financial planners, corporate tax preparers, auditors and auditing managers, statistical analysts, general managers, loan officers, and more. Part-time positions are available for tax preparers and bank tellers, although these positions may also be available on a full-time basis.

You may even wish to do individual and corporate tax returns from your home or become a personal assistant for individuals or small businesses that need someone to take care of their finances.

Social Services

Social service agencies have a variety of positions in various occupations, ranging from health care to children's services to government programs. These positions typically are not high paying, but they can be personally rewarding and may offer the flexibility to fit your lifestyle.

Social workers, counselors, social service managers, administrative assistants, and aides are needed in various organizations to assess, support, and treat patients and their families. Instructional planners, aides, and curriculum writers are also needed, depending on the field. Full- and part-time positions are available at agencies and for in-home counseling and support.

Some positions in the social service agencies require minimal education, while others require an advanced degree in the field or specialty you are considering. You may also be required to obtain background checks. Consult with the agency or organization for which you would like to work to learn of the requirements for openings.

Recreation and Hospitality

Do you like to travel? How about becoming a tour host or guide for a local or long distance bus tour company? As the population ages, more people have time to travel, take tours, and attend recreational activities. A variety of positions are available in a number of different areas ranging from tour guide to travel agent to travel writer to activities director to travel consultant.

Some places to search for jobs in this industry are at various airlines and airports, hotels and motels, travel agencies, tour operators, tour wholesalers, local and state tourism offices, motor coach and rail companies, car rental companies, sports arenas, casinos, cruise lines, and state or national parks.

A sampling of positions available in the recreation and hospitality industries include airline reservationists, travel reservationists, gate agents, immigration agents, customs agents, security personnel, hotel auditors, front desk reservationists, housekeepers, tour guides and directors, travel agents and planners, food and beverage managers, customer service representatives, sales representatives, managers, bus drivers, travel writers and brochure designers, drivers, cleaners, and the like.

A bed and breakfast or a family-owned inn is another viable option for individuals who are interested in owning and running their own business in the hospitality industry. These B&Bs and inns are located all over the country (and world) in small and large towns and cities.

A specialized area of the hospitality and recreation field is the resort. Specialized resorts include a variety of activities such as ski and golf and offer a variety of facilities, such as those that cater to honeymooners. Resorts can be found in mountain, country, city, ocean, and island locations.

Conventions

Conventions and conferences are big business for companies who send their employees for training, education, and annual meetings. These conventions require the skills of meeting planners, customer service representatives, facility managers, marketing and public relations directors, sales managers, banquet captains, travel agents, and so forth.

If you enjoy working in the food industry, convention centers often employ food preparers and buyers, caterers, chefs, servers, managers, and banquet captains.

Freelance Writing

Freelance writers are needed for newspapers, magazines, textbooks, newsletters, Ezines, brochures, websites, companies, non-profits, government agencies, associations, schools, churches, and the like.

You could become a technical writer on a full-time or project basis where you write product manuals and instructions that are less technical so the average person can understand them. You may find a job writing company policy and procedures manuals, advertising brochures, sales letters, and other corporate documents.

If you enjoy dining out, you can be paid to write restaurant reviews for online services. If you are an avid reader, you can write book reviews for magazines and newspapers. Travelers can write reviews for places they have visited.

If you have excellent written communication skills, you may want to consider a freelance writing career. A creative writing class or journalism class at a local college will improve your writing skills and bring you current in today's writing style. Join a professional writers group or a critique group, and attend conferences. If you cannot travel to meetings and conferences, many writing associations offer online courses and critique groups. Read the type of material you would like to write to get a sense of what to write and how to do it properly.

In addition to writing, freelancers can become proofreaders or editors on a full- or part-time basis. Much of this work can be done in your home.

Party, Event, and Wedding Planning

Special events are big business and take place year round. People and businesses who do not want the stress and hassle of planning for a wedding, retirement, reception, birthday party, anniversary party, grand opening celebration, annual meeting, and other special occasions hire event planners to take care of the dozens of details involved in such an event.

Planners may be responsible for creating and sending invitations, securing a suitable location, ordering flowers, deciding on the menu, scheduling and setting up the entertainment and music, planning games and activities, acquiring favors and treats, ordering giveaways, arranging transportation, suggesting proper attire and arranging fittings, and so forth.

Some people prefer to provide services and products to an event planner instead of actually becoming an event planner, such as florists, crafters, entertainers, and the like.

Miscellaneous Jobs

In addition to the various industries and possible positions discussed in this chapter, be aware that many other opportunities exist for older workers. You will only be limited by your imagination. Consider the following jobs:

- Do you love animals? Would you enjoy being a veterinarian, pet sitter or walker, groomer, pet store clerk or owner, or a pet photographer? All of these positions are excellent for older workers. If you do not need a paycheck, you could volunteer at a pet shelter in any number of positions.

- Do you like to write lessons and train people but are unsure you want to become a teacher? How about becoming a textbook writer or reviewer, a proofreader, or a curriculum specialist?

- Do you like to golf? Seek a position at one of the thousands of golf courses, where you can not only use your skills but also take advantage of perks the course offers employees. If you prefer another sport, there are sports arenas and activity centers everywhere that offer a variety of positions. For instance, you could sharpen skates or clean the ice at the local skating arena or take care of a baseball or football field at a stadium.

- Do you like to bake? Why not become a baker for the local bake shop, catering company, mall cookie shop, or restaurant? You may even want to build a home-based baking or catering business.

- Do you have a hobby or like to do crafts? Consider a position in a hobby shop that specializes in your interest ,or teach your hobby skill privately or at your local community college, at a vocational-technical school, for an adult education program, or in a craft store. You do not even need teaching credentials to become a hobby teacher, and many stores and adult education programs welcome proposals for new classes. Ceramics, tole painting, pottery, flower arranging, crocheting, scrapbooking, cooking, fabric design and sewing, dancing—the list of hobbies you can teach to others is endless.

- Do you like cars? In addition to car sales, you could look into car detailing, financing cars, repairs, body work, and parts selling. You might want to consider working at a race track or a car auction center.

- Do you like make-up and present a polished appearance? Work out of your home selling cosmetics, or take a job at a department store cosmetic counter or in a beauty salon. In addition, you could become a color consultant and advise clients of the best colors for their features.

- Do you like gardening and flowers? Nurseries, flower shops, and home and garden centers, and conservatories need landscapers, flower arrangers, horticulturists, and other types of workers who are well-informed about their products and excited to work in the field. Many grocery stores and craft supply stores have floral departments as well.

- Do you have a flair for taking pictures? A photography career may be for you, either as an independent photographer or one with a company. You could get paid to take pictures of wildlife and birds for magazines, weddings and special events, or children and pets.

- Does a fun environment appeal to you? Theme parks, museums, science centers, zoos, theaters, and the like need employees of all kinds. Remember, all these places have accounting, sales, advertising, marketing, administrative, and management positions.

- Are you concerned about the environment? Consider becoming an air or water pollution control specialist, energy conservationist, or working in any number of the new green jobs.

- Do you like to shop? You can get paid to shop by becoming a secret shopper for various stores.

- How are your computer and Internet skills? Become a web designer, online retailer, IT researcher or analyst, or a virtual assistant to someone who is too busy to complete all of her tasks.

Instead of applying for a traditional job, use your imagination and creative skills to land an exciting, enjoyable job in a fun environment or create one of your own.

Summary

With all of the available information for age 50-plus job seekers, arm yourself in the best possible way to conduct your job search and to find employment that you will enjoy for years to come.

Much of your success will depend on the field and type of work you want, as well as the type of position—full- or part-time, flexible hours, or project basis. Doing appropriate research will direct you to the right position.

Your attitude, personality, and professional image influence employers, customers, and clients. Sell your work ethic, experience, productivity level, and people skills to the employer.

Check local zoning laws and restrictions for operating a home-based business and tax laws and other legal concerns when you produce income from self-employment.

CHAPTER 8

CREATE A SUCCESS PLAN

Countless people say they want to be successful, but the real questions are: What does success mean to you? How badly do you want to succeed? Are you willing to do whatever it takes to attain what you consider to be successful? Success demands hard work, self-discipline, and an enormous amount of time. Success often means moving out of an established comfort zone, motivating yourself again and again, taking time to focus on goals, pushing yourself even when you do not want to keep going, eliminating decades-old habits, and persisting until you achieve the results you want. All of this takes tremendous commitment and effort and the will and ability to keep going amid disappointment.

To achieve what you want, you will need to create a success plan. This plan begins with goal setting. Your goal will lead to the development of a plan, a map of sorts, to get you where you want to go. Although goals should encompass all areas of your life to create balance, this book is devoted only to the goals related to finding and attaining a job, especially for the mature worker. The information, example goals, tips, and sample forms included in this chapter reflect that intention.

Although unemployment is high and layoffs are everywhere, some companies are still hiring and people are still getting jobs. Instead of complaining that there are no good jobs, take the actions, explained in this chapter, necessary to find one, or else create a job of your own by going into business for yourself.

As an older person looking for work, you may need to be more committed than younger job seekers because, on average, it takes people over the age of 50 longer to find a job. That does not mean there is no job for you, just that you should prepare yourself for a search that may last for several months. You also may want to choose realistic options like those presented in Chapter 7, "Who's Hiring?" such as working for a small business.

If you want to succeed in finding a job, you must be willing to put everything you have into the job search for as long as it takes to get the position you want. This is not an easy task in an economy such as this one that sheds jobs faster than it replaces them. Setting goals, writing them down, and taking consistent action to reach them can help. In addition, you will want to constantly remind yourself why you set the goal and what you hope to accomplish by achieving it. Constant attention to the goal and high expectations will give you the confidence you need to reach the goal.

You must take the initiative to do whatever is necessary—research, write a resume, practice your interviewing skills, and all the other topics covered in this book, to be successful. You cannot wait for someone to come to you with a job offer. Look for opportunities and follow up on every possibility you come across.

Mature job seekers face many obstacles during the job hunt. Some of these obstacles were discussed throughout this book, as were ideas on how to deal with or eliminate them. Persevere by focusing on what is possible. Train your mind to look for solutions.

Now, the question becomes, how committed are you to finding a job? Discipline yourself to work every day to find a suitable position. Incorporate the ideas discussed in previous chapters of this book into your plan, and then do what you have to do to find a job. Expect to find the right position for you. Ignore distractions and motivate yourself to take action even when you do not feel like it. Re-invent yourself if necessary to adapt to available jobs. Sell yourself to company decision makers. Follow up on every resume you send and every interview you conduct. Seek the support of friends to keep your self-esteem high, which will reinforce your willingness to work at finding a job. Celebrate successes such as joining an online networking group or learning a new skill. These celebrations will motivate you to achieve more.

To test your commitment level, ask yourself if you are willing to take the following steps and keep taking them until you reach your goal:

- Research companies online, in newspapers and journals, and through network contacts.
- Research industries and fields of interest.
- Attend meetings and events where you can interact with current network contacts and add new individuals to your list.
- Call friends in your network to chat and remind them you are still looking for a job.
- Update skills or learn new ones.
- Learn the latest technology.
- Go back to school.
- Write a resume using current formatting and keywords.
- Post resumes to online employment sites and company websites.
- Send a hundred resumes or more.
- Join LinkedIn and Facebook.
- Tweet for a job.
- Let go of out-dated notions.
- Interview with a much younger interviewer.
- Be willing to work for a much younger supervisor.
- Be open-minded and flexible.
- Be positive and energetic.
- Update your professional image.
- Persist until you are successful.

If it seems like a lot of work to find a job, that is because it is. It has been said that finding a job is a job in itself. Therefore, you must be willing to put as much time and effort into your search as you would give to an actual employer. An hour or two here and there will likely not bring success.

Some people who have been let go from companies have given up in this poor economy without even trying to find another position. They simply believe there are no jobs to be had. Some have opted for retirement following a layoff or firing, figuring no one would hire them at their age. Others have sent a dozen or more resumes via mail or posted a few resumes online and then have complained that no one is hiring because they never received a response to their employment letters. Still others have sent a hundred or more resumes and then have quit doing so when they failed to get a job.

All of these examples show how easy it is to give up the search for a job and how difficult it is to continue searching in the face of extreme odds. Sometimes success is elusive, but by persisting you stand a good chance of winning. You may have to persist, though, for a long, long time. To assist you in keeping on track and remaining persistent, set goals and make a plan that you can stick to even during unproductive times. Track your successful steps toward your goal to keep motivation and commitment strong. Line up supporters who will cheer you on when your enthusiasm wanes during your search or due to potential job rejections.

Make your job search goals and plan of action a culmination of all of the things discussed throughout this book from assessing your skills and abilities to searching for a job to writing a resume and posting it online to interviewing.

Set Job Search Goals

A goal helps you control your situation by giving you a specific target to aim for and a defined time period to hit it. A goal defines what it is that you want and sets the course so that you move toward those wants. The goal should be the result of the careful consideration of what you want stated in positive terms. It should be something you are passionate enough about that you will expend the necessary energy on it, and the goal should be yours alone. When your goal hinges on other people, you have a strike against you, because you have no control over anyone but yourself. You can ask people to help you reach your goals, but you cannot make them act in a certain way so that you do reach them.

Set the Goal. Make the most of your job search efforts by setting a main career goal (finding a job) and working every day toward achieving it. Begin by thinking about what you want to accomplish in very specific terms. Saying you want a job is not specific enough. Try: I want to obtain a sales position with a small business, making $45,000 per year with benefits. If you have a particular company in mind that you would like to work for, including that information will narrow your goal even further and make it more personal for you. The more specific and personal the goal, the more likely it is that you will go after it with a dedication and commitment that will produce the results you want.

Figure Out the Benefits. Next, fix in your mind why you want the goal and the benefits you will gain when you attain it. For example, lots of people want jobs. However, saying that finding a job will give you the money and benefits you need to live will bolster your self-esteem and will give you a satisfying feeling of contributing to society, is something that will fuel your personal commitment to attain it. Having a good reason for wanting the goal will motivate you and keep you engaged in the attainment of the goal.

Be Practical. A successful goal must be practical. Declaring that you want an administrative assistant position in a small company making $120,000 per year is unrealistic for most people. Keep it realistic, although you do want the goal to be somewhat challenging to make it worth the effort. However, if the goal is so challenging that you do not believe you can reasonably attain it, you probably will not (1) focus on it, (2) put the energy and enthusiasm into achieving it, (3) take the steps you need to be successful, or (4) persist. Making the goal personal will drive you to attain it.

Be Timely. Set a deadline for achieving your goal by estimating how long you can reasonably expect to take to reach the goal. Write the deadline on a calendar and look at it periodically. Without a deadline, your goal could hang in limbo and never be accomplished. A deadline holds you accountable for taking the necessary action, in a timely manner, toward reaching the goal. It creates the kind of urgency that will get results. Telling the deadline to individuals who support your efforts will hold you even more accountable.

Measure It. Make your goal measurable so you will know if and when you have achieved it. Using a quantitative measurement makes it easy to see where you are and how far you need to go. For example, saying you would like to have a sales position with a small company, making $45,000 and to be hired within six months (or by an actual date) is measurable. You know what you want, where you want it, when you want it, and how much money you want to make.

Setting secondary goals of searching want ads and websites or writing a resume is also measurable. You can gauge your progress as you complete secondary goals and keep track of what you have accomplished and be able to see what more you need to do to reach your main goal of finding the job you desire. If you do not reach your goal within the time period you have set, you can set another deadline or eliminate the goal if it is no longer viable.

Be Specific. Include every possible detail about your goal. When you make goals specific, you know exactly what you want and can, therefore, figure out what it will take to reach them, or you can find someone who can assist you. Then, you can set about creating a suitable plan that will help you reach the goal. You are also more likely to focus on goals if they are specific. You will be able to go after them with a single-minded approach, avoiding the myriad distractions that could keep you from attaining them.

Make your job search goal-specific by asking yourself questions such as the following:

- In what industry or occupation do you want to work?
- In what company would you like to work?
- What type of position do you want?
- What duties would you like to perform?
- Do you have the skills and abilities to perform this job?
- Where do you want this position to be located?
- Do you want to work full time, part time, or on a project basis?
- What salary are you willing to accept?
- What other criteria do you have for accepting a job?
- When would you like to begin this job?

The answers to the preceding questions can assist you in setting appropriate, positive goals that will turn wishful thinking into an action-packed attempt to attain what you want. To get an idea of how specific you should be, look at the sample goal on the next page.

Take Charge

Set a specific, practical, measurable main goal for getting a job. Figure out a time-frame for the goal and a deadline. Write down all of the benefits you will receive when you attain your goal. Fill in the information for your main goal in the blank sample goal form provided on the next page.

Sample Goal

Goal: To find a sales position with a small business, making $45,000 per year with benefits.

This goal is important to me because: I will be able to pay living expenses and enjoy traveling. I will be able to buy and care for a nice home. I will be a contributing member of society.

Specifics and measurability: I want a full-time position, using my current skills and abilities, making $45,000 per year with full medical benefits, located close to my home, and in a small business environment.

Timeframe: I would like to acquire this position within three months from today.

Deadline Date: _____

My Goal

Goal: _____
_____

This goal is important to me because: _____
_____
_____

Specifics and measurability: _____
_____
_____
_____

Timeframe: _____
_____

Deadline Date: _____

When you set a major goal (for example, to get a job), you may want to set secondary goals that break down that major goal (for example, research companies or prepare a resume), and then list steps to attain each goal (for example, go online to research company websites, find a current resume format to use, and learn keywords of the industry). Secondary goals can serve as benchmarks that show your progress (or lack thereof).

Take a look at the following chart to see how a main goal can be broken down into spin-off goals, also known as secondary goals. Each of those secondary goals can then be broken down further into the individual steps you will need to take and the tasks you will need to complete.

If your main goal is to find a job, you can see from the chart that there is a lot to the process. Each of the subcategories under the goal to find a job become secondary goals to help you make your main goal attainable. The secondary goals listed in the example support the main goal of finding a job by pinpointing how to reach it. From these secondary goals, there are many steps and individual tasks that will help you achieve the goal. Determining individual steps to take is discussed in the next section in this chapter, which is entitled Create an Action Plan.

Main and Secondary Goals

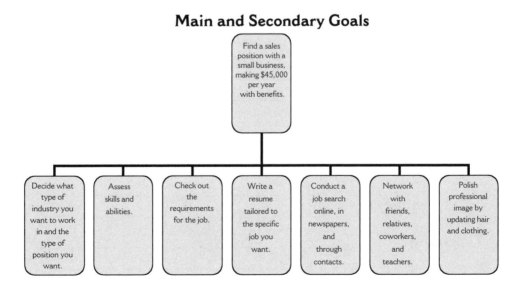

A main goal that is broken down into manageable parts will provide the criteria you need to determine if you are on the right path and if you are progressing as you desire. Your subconscious will be open to attaining the goal, rather than creating doubts and sabotaging your efforts because of lack of focus.

Each secondary goal aimed at your main goal of finding a job should also be specific, practical, measurable, written, and have a timeframe. Tie each goal to action steps. By breaking down the main goal, you avoid becoming overwhelmed and stuck in "I don't know what to do" mode. You can easily do one task or take one step at a time.

It is likely you will encounter obstacles while working toward your goals. Brainstorm potential obstacles you might encounter and some creative solutions to overcoming them. When obstacles do arise, analyze them to develop a strategy to remove them or else look for a way to go around them. Enlist the help of people from your network to find solutions to problems.

Remember, everyone has setbacks; everyone has difficulties. Keep going in the face of adversity. Do not criticize yourself for lack of progress or failure to take necessary steps. Adjust the goal and timeframe, work harder at focusing on the goal, and take action on what you have been avoiding. If procrastination is the problem, figure out why you are procrastinating, and get yourself back on track as soon as possible.

Review your goals every day, evaluate the progress of each step you take, and make a note of when each secondary goal is reached. Challenge yourself. Are you proceeding as planned? Is there something more you can do? Is this goal still a priority?

If what you have done to reach the goal does not turn out as planned, change your tactics. Ask yourself what you can do differently to achieve the results you want. Then do it if you want to change the results you have been getting up until this point. Keep doing what has worked and eliminate or adjust what does not work. Ask for help from your support network whenever you need it.

Review these goal setting tips.

Goal Setting Tips

- State your goals in specific terms; be clear about what you want.
- Use positive language.
- Determine why you want to attain the goal.
- Be realistic about what you can achieve.
- Set a deadline for achieving the goals; again, be realistic.
- Determine the criteria you will use to measure whether you are successful at attaining the goal.
- Break your main goal into smaller goals or steps.
- Create a plan for achieving your goals by writing down the individual steps you will need to take for the main and secondary goals.
- List obstacles you might encounter while striving for your goal.
- Brainstorm solutions for overcoming obstacles.
- Check your daily progress.
- Evaluate your progress toward achieving goals and adjust as necessary.
- Commit to achieving goals and do whatever it takes to reach them.
- Enlist the help of a support group.
- Persist no matter what.

Take Charge

Think about the secondary goals you will need to establish in order to get to your main goal. Take the preceding list of goal tips into consideration when making decisions about the goals you will set. Write your main goal and secondary goals in the following chart. Add secondary goal boxes as needed or eliminate the extra ones.

Main and Secondary Goals

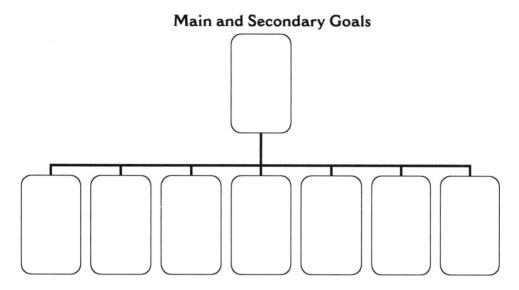

Constantly remind yourself what the payoff will be when you reach your goal and why you want it. Whether you take action or not and the type of action you take will determine whether you reach your goals.

Take Charge

Think about each of the goals you have set for yourself and answer the following questions. Your answers will help you determine whether the goal is one you will fully commit to and benefit from attaining.

- What will you gain by reaching this goal?
- Is the goal realistic?
- Is this your goal and no one else's goal?
- Is the timeframe realistic?
- What do you need to do to reach this goal?
- Do you have the skills and abilities to do what you need to do to reach this goal?
- Are you willing to do whatever is necessary to attain the proper credentials and job skills for the position you want?
- Are you committed to doing whatever you need to do for as long as needed to reach this goal?

- Do you know anyone at the company for which you would like to work that you can network with to obtain information on a position or who can give you a referral for a position?

- What problems are you likely to encounter while taking steps toward achieving this goal?

- Is there someone or something that can help you overcome problems you may encounter while taking steps toward achieving this goal?

- What are the specific steps and tasks that you can take to reach this goal?

Create an Action Plan

Once you have decided what you want to achieve and have established your goals, it is time to do something about it. As with any sizeable, important project, you need an action plan to put your job search goals into play. A realistic strategy is a must. Think about what steps you can take to attain your goals. How are you going to do them? Can you break those steps down into smaller tasks to keep from attempting too much at once? Set daily goals so you can see that you are moving forward. How will you know when the goal is reached? Establish criteria, assign a deadline to each step, and post the deadlines where you can see them. Make outcomes tangible and you will be able to see results. Successful results will propel you forward and increase your self-esteem.

It is not enough to want to find a job and write down that goal. You must take action every day toward getting that job even if it is something simple like sending out another resume or calling another networking contact. Do what you need to do. There can be no excuses such as "I do not know what steps to take" or "I do not have the time to look for a job" or "There are no jobs." Write down where you want to devote your time and energy every day.

Create a doable action plan for attaining your goals by breaking your main goal into secondary goals and then by breaking those goals into daily and weekly steps you can take. This process sets up an action plan that marks the way to your goal. Lay out the steps and tasks in order of priority and in a logical progression.

Take a look at the steps listed in the following sample goal and action steps box:

Sample Goal and Action Steps

Goal: To find a sales position with a small business, making $45,000 per year with benefits.

This goal is important to me because: I will be able to pay living expenses and enjoy traveling. I will be able to buy and care for a nice home. I will be a contributing member of society.

Specifics and measurability: I want a full-time position, using my current skills and abilities, making $45,000 per year with full medical benefits, located close to my home, and in a small business environment.

Timeframe: I would like to acquire this position within three months from today.

Deadline Date: _____

Action Steps to Take to Find a Company and Position:

1. Assess skills and abilities to determine what positions I can fill and where I need improvement.
2. Assess my personal characteristics.
3. Research local small businesses to determine openings and requirements.
   a. Determine skill and ability requirements.
   b. Determine education and experience requirements.
   c. Determine size of company and location.
   d. Determine salary and benefits.
   e. Determine whether my skills and abilities match the job requirements.
4. List areas where I need improvement.
5. Obtain training or additional skills needed to meet job requirements.
6. Network with contacts to determine if anyone knows someone within the company to which I want to send resumes.
7. Prepare a resume tailored to the company and position desired.

8. Obtain feedback on resume from friends and coworkers.

9. Write a cover letter tailored to the position and obtain feedback on the letter.

10. Send tailored resumes to appropriate companies.

11. Post resumes on appropriate company websites.

12. Create a method for tracking where resumes are sent.

13. Contact references and ask permission to use their names.

14. Prepare a reference sheet.

15. Practice answers to typical interview questions.

16. Do mock interviews with a friend.

17. Review accomplishments and prepare examples.

18. Put together a portfolio.

19. Schedule interviews and record appropriate information including date, time, location, and title and name of interviewer.

20. Dress professionally for the interview, arrive on time, greet everyone courteously, listen carefully to the interviewer, respond properly and enthusiastically to questions, ask appropriate questions, give specific examples of projects and accomplishments with measurable results, ask for the job, and thank the interviewer.

21. Send thank you letters after interviewing.

22. Follow up interviews with a phone call if necessary.

23. Network, network, network.

Many of the preceding steps could be broken down further into smaller steps. For instance, Step 5 "Obtain training or additional skills to meet job requirements," could be broken down to include the steps you would take to obtain the training: (1) researching schools, (2) contacting the school's admissions office, (3) arrange method of payment for training, (4) enrolling in a course, and (5) taking the course. As you can see, pursuing a goal on a task-by-task basis makes it doable.

Each goal and secondary goal, along with the steps you take to reach it, should be written on a separate action plan sheet like the one that follows. The sample action plan that follows is written for the secondary goal of writing a resume that is part of the main goal of finding a job.

Action Plan for Writing a Resume

Goal: To write a resume   **Deadline**: Four days

Step 1: Find examples of current resumes.

      Date Completed: _____

    Tasks: (1) Search online, read resume books, seek advice from
           contacts.
          (2) Choose appropriate format.
          (3) Isolate keywords and requirements from job description.

Step 2: Determine what to include on the resume.

      Date Completed: _____

    Tasks: (1) Match background and abilities to job requirements.
          (2) Prioritize information.

Step 3: Write the resume.

      Date Completed: _____

    Tasks: (1) Proofread resume.
          (2) Have resume critiqued and proofread by network
            contacts.
          (3) Print resumes on resume grade paper for sending via
            mail, and post resumes to company and employment
            websites.

Potential Obstacles:

    (1) Cannot find the job requirements for the position I want.

    (2) Do not know how to post a resume online.

    (3) Resume is too long because of too much information.

Possible Solutions:

    (1) Search for similar positions; ask network contacts if they know
       of the company and its requirements.

    (2) Ask for help from network contacts who can put your resume
       online; find a tutor to learn how to prepare and submit online
       resumes.

    (3) Eliminate information unrelated to the position; limit years of
       experience listed on the resume.

Take Charge

Keep a daily or weekly record of your progress toward achieving the goals you set. Use the following action plan form to write your goal of finding a job and the subsequent steps to achieve it. Fill in individual tasks for each step. You should complete an action plan for your main goal and for each of your secondary ones.

Action Plan for Writing a Resume

Goal: _____   **Deadline**: _____

Step 1: _____

    Date Completed: _____

    Tasks: (1) _____

           (2) _____

           (3) _____

Step 2: _____

    Date Completed: _____

    Tasks: (1) _____

           (2) _____

           (3) _____

Step 3: _____

    Date Completed: _____

    Tasks: (1) _____

           (2) _____

           (3) _____

Potential Obstacles:

    (1) _____

    (2) _____

    (3) _____

Possible Solutions:

    (1) _____

    (2) _____

    (3) _____

As with any plan, things sometimes go wrong. Expect the unexpected, and be adaptable when the unexpected comes. Allow yourself options.

After you determine the steps you need to take toward the achievement of your goal, create a to-do list and prioritize the tasks on it. A simple 1-2-3 or A-B-C system should suffice for ranking the priority order of the tasks as Urgent, Important, and Not Important. For instance, if you have an interview, that will be a 1 or an A on your to-do list—the highest priority for the day of the interview.

If you are not in the habit of using a to-do list, you might consider the effectiveness of using one to monitor your progress toward your goals. Your to-do list will remind you what you need to do so you are not wasting time on trivial tasks. The to-do list can show you how much time it will take per day to complete each step and subsequent tasks toward reaching your goal. In addition, crossing items off the to-do list as you complete them is a morale booster.

To-Do List

Date _____

1. Go to bookstore and buy a resume-writing book.
2. Read through the resumes and find ones suited to the position I want. Check the keywords and other pertinent information.
3. Decide on a format to use for my resume.

Take the Time

Make the time to search for a job. Given the realities of this job market, you will need to expend a lot of time on your job search. Prepare yourself to put in the time needed.

Review the time management tips in Chapter 5 "Attitude, Energy, and Dressing for Success," and then find and eliminate time wasters that could keep you from your goal. At the end of the day, ask yourself if you have spent your time wisely focused on your goals.

Think about your answers to the following questions and decide if you are willing and able to take the necessary steps.

- What is the first thing I need to do to reach this goal?
- Am I willing to take that step to reach my goal?
- Do I have the skills and abilities to take the step?
- How long will it take me to complete the step?
- Am I willing to spend the time required to complete the step?
- What is the next thing I need to do to reach this goal?
- Am I willing to take the next step to reach my goal?
- Do I have the skills and abilities to take the step?
- How long will it take me to complete the step?
- Am I willing to spend the time required to complete the step?

Determine how you are spending your time now and how you can adjust it to include the hours necessary for your job search. Write down the typical hours in your day and jot down what you can do each hour to reach job search goals.

Use a simple calendar or list like the one below to track your time.

How Do I Spend My Time?		
Time	What did I do?	Was it productive?
6:00–7:00 a.m.		
7:00–8:00 a.m.		
8:00–9:00 a.m.		
9:00–10:00 a.m.		

Make a list of time wasters and decide if you can eliminate any of them. Remember to include on your list people who waste your time as well as the activities that waste it. Eliminate or minimize time wasters and then block out enough time for reaching each of your goals.

Time Wasters

Time waster: _____

_____

Can it be eliminated? If not, why not? _____

_____

_____

Time waster: _____

_____

Can it be eliminated? If not, why not? _____

_____

_____

Take Charge

After answering the preceding questions, determine how you will spend your time during your job search. Wisely schedule your time in order to complete your goals. Analyze where your time is going and make a list of time wasters and ways to eliminate them. Create a daily to-do list of the tasks you will need to complete in order to reach your goals. Block out the time necessary to complete the goals.

Write a Resume

After assessing your abilities and background as discussed in Chapter 1, "What Skills and Qualifications Set You Apart," decide on the type of position you are qualified for and would like to obtain. Analyze the requirements for the position and write a resume slanted to that particular job following the tips provided in Chapter 2, "Resumes and Employment Letters." Include on your resume the keywords and the duties mentioned in the job description or on the company website. Review the keyword and action verb lists in Chapter 2 for example words.

If there is no job description for a position you desire, research similar positions and incorporate the details and keywords from the descriptions of those jobs.

Decide on the best resume format to use for your particular circumstances—chronological, functional, or combination. Choose the best arrangement for your information, depending upon your circumstances and the job requirements. Prioritize your information by employment history, skills and abilities, education, and accomplishments.

Read over the following items. Use your answers to determine what information to include on your resume:

- Which previous positions and titles have you held that should be included?
- What previous experience should you include?
- Write a qualifications summary that aligns with the position you want.
- Detail your technical experience and software skills.
- List your transferable skills that will complement the position for which you are applying.
- Decide which action verbs will best represent your skills and abilities.
- Find keywords in the job description and those used in the industry and include them on your resume.
- List quantified achievements—measurable results you have accomplished.
- Describe the value you added to previous employers.
- Describe major projects you worked on and the results achieved.
- List your responsibilities at previous positions.
- Detail your education, training, and certification.
- List your activities, awards, letters, and proof of achievements.

Line Up References

Use the guidelines given in Chapter 2 to select three to five appropriate individuals to use as professional references. Contact these individuals to reconnect or, if needed, to refresh their minds about how you know each other. Ask permission to use their names as job references.

Before giving a reference's name to a perspective employer, be certain the reference will give a glowing account of your work history and/or abilities. If you have any doubt the individual will give you a good reference, select a different person.

Put Together a Portfolio

Showcase your accomplishments by putting together a portfolio of samples of your work, projects you have completed, letters of recommendation, awards, certifications, positive employment evaluations, volunteer projects, and anything else that will impress perspective employers. You may want to make a video of a presentation that you gave to include in your portfolio or create an online portfolio.

Choose a professional-looking leather portfolio or briefcase to hold your documentation for your interviews.

Some items to include in a portfolio include the following:

- Copies of your resume and reference sheet on bond paper
- Sample projects you worked on and/or completed
- Samples of various tasks you performed
- Letters of recommendation
- Positive letters and emails from customers, clients, and supervisors
- Publications
- Awards
- Positive annual performance reviews
- Copies of degrees, diplomas, and certifications
- Videos or hard copies of presentations you gave
- An image of your website

Take Charge

Create a portfolio to showcase your accomplishments. Purchase a leather portfolio or briefcase to store your documentation. Present the portfolio at your interviews.

Track Your Research

Research the industry in which you would like to work to find companies you prefer to work for and the job requirements for any openings. (See Chapter 3, "Using Technology to Find Employment.") This information will help you to know which employers are looking for someone with your qualifications so you will know what to include on a resume and in a portfolio. It will also allow you to match your particular talents with each company's requirements.

In addition to general research information, such as types of positions in the field and salaries for similar jobs, look for information on individual companies' phone numbers, addresses, driving directions, parking facilities and costs, interviewers' names and titles, names and titles of high-ranking company executives, and products and services the company provides.

Keep a written record of your research and organize it so you will be able to utilize it again and again when applying for jobs. Use a table like the one below, a notebook, or an electronic spreadsheet or calendar.

Companies Researched		
Company Researched	Website Address	Information

Take Charge

Keep a written record of your research. Decide what method you will use to record and organize the information you gather.

When you send resumes or post them online, be sure to record where you sent them and the date sent. It is easy to forget key information whenever you send a number of resumes if you do not record the information.

Information can be recorded in a notebook, on index cards, in an electronic file or spreadsheet, on a calendar, or by other means. Use a system that works for you. The following table details the type of information you might want to record.

Where I Sent Resumes				
Company Name	Address	Telephone Number	Date Resume Application Sent/Interview	Response

When you schedule an interview, record that information, too. You will want to record the company name and address, the correct name and title of the interviewer, and the date and time of the interview. Fill in your thoughts about how the interview went and any follow-up on your part or the company's.

Record of Interviews					
Company Name	Address	Telephone Number	Date of Interview	Results	Follow-up

Take Charge

Maintain a record of where you have sent resumes and the dates they were sent. Create a system that works for you and keep it up to date throughout your job search.

Increase Your Success at Achieving Goals

What can you do to increase your success at achieving your goals? Set goals that you are passionate about so they will dominate your thoughts and actions and you will have the enthusiasm to carry them through. Ask yourself why you want the goal, and think about how you will benefit from attaining it. Write down the goals and the benefits of working on the goals and of attaining the goals. What advantages will the goals bring? What will you have when you have reached the goals? How will you feel after having achieved the goals?

In addition to the goal setting techniques presented throughout this chapter, make a commitment to achieve your goals no matter what it takes. When you are 100 percent committed, you will do whatever is necessary no matter how difficult or monotonous it may seem. Sending resumes day after day can become a repetitive, boring task, especially when it seems you are not making any headway toward your goal. With a strong enough desire, you will do it anyway until you succeed.

Keep your enthusiasm high by focusing on your goal, which is to be offered a job that you want. Never give up. Face setbacks and take the necessary risks. Look at difficulties, such as searching for openings and positing resumes online, as challenges. Find creative ways to solve obstacles you incur. When you need assistance or a helping hand, you can always call on someone from your support group to help you.

Avoid procrastination; take action, no matter how difficult the step. Sometimes we feel we do not know what to do. In such instances, do something anyway. Get rid of the doubts that undermine your taking action, and remove the desire to be idle. Move from your comfort zone and challenge yourself. Put yourself out there and try new things. If something you tried does not work, try a different approach. Be flexible. Things are in a constant state of change, and the only way to grow is to change with them.

Look at what you are doing and modify your approach when what you are doing does not work. This might entail setting new secondary goals or changing the steps you are taking to reach the ones you have already set.

Another way to remain committed is to look at the consequences of not reaching your goal. What will happen? That answer may be enough to encourage you to take action where and when you need to do so. Avoid negative thoughts and doubts.

Visualize Success

Picture yourself sitting behind the desk in your new office. Imagine talking to clients about arranging their trips. See yourself selling products and services. Whatever type of work you are seeking, get a clear picture of yourself performing the tasks associated with it. Make it so real that it seems you are already in the position.

By visualizing success, you will have a constant awareness of what you are reaching for and what it will feel like when you get there. Hopefully, that will enrich your commitment.

Get the Most Out of Your Job Search

It is time to put together a job search plan and pull out all the stops. There can be no whining, no complaining, no excuses, and no procrastination. Begin with the goal of finding a job and take steps everyday to achieve it. If you feel you cannot do what is required, get a cheerleader. Find someone to coach you and walk you through the steps. Ask someone to hold you accountable for sending those resumes. You will not get anywhere if you do not take action.

Use the following forms to lay out what you have to do and to keep yourself organized while doing it.

Goal Sheet

Goal: _____

_____

This goal is important to me because:_____

_____

This goal is realistic because:_____

_____

This is how I can measure this goal: _____

_____

_____

Timeframe for reaching this goal: _____

Deadline to reach goal: _____

Main and Secondary Goals

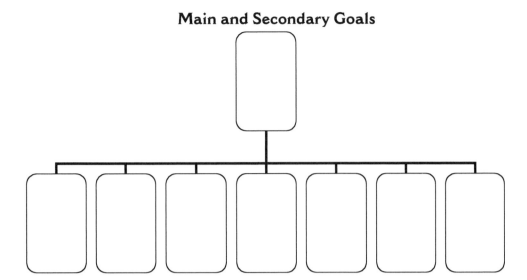

Action Plan for Goals

Step 1: _____
_____
_____

    Tasks: (a) _____
                 (b) _____
                 (c) _____

Step 2: _____
_____
_____

    Tasks: (a) _____
                 (b) _____
                 (c) _____

Step 3: _____
_____
_____

    Tasks: (a) _____
                 (b) _____
                 (c) _____

Step 4: _____

_____

_____

    Tasks: (a) _____

          (b) _____

          (c) _____

Step 5: _____

_____

_____

    Tasks: (a) _____

          (b) _____

          (c) _____

Potential obstacles:

_____

_____

_____

_____

_____

Strategies to eliminate obstacles:

_____

_____

_____

_____

_____

_____

_____

Companies Researched		
Company Researched	Website Address	Information

Where I Sent Resumes				
Company Name	Address	Telephone Number	Date Resume Application Sent/Interview	Response

Record of Interviews					
Company Name	Address	Telephone Number	Date of Interview	Results	Follow-up

How Do I Spend My Time?		
Time	What did I do?	Was it productive?
6:00-7:00 a.m.		
7:00-8:00 a.m.		
8:00-9:00 a.m.		
9:00-10:00 a.m.		
10:00-11:00 a.m.		
11:00-12:00 noon		
12:00-1:00 p.m.		
1:00-2:00 p.m.		
2:00-3:00 p.m.		
3:00-4:00 p.m.		
4:00-5:00 p.m.		
5:00-6:00 p.m.		
6:00-7:00 p.m.		
7:00-8:00 p.m.		
8:00-9:00 p.m.		
9:00-10:00 p.m.		
10:00-11:00 p.m.		
11:00-12:00 p.m.		

Summary

If you are 50 or older and want to find a job, realize the challenges ahead of you and meet them. Set goals and create a plan of the steps you can take to achieve your goals. Commit 100 percent to doing whatever it takes to succeed.

Organize your job search by documenting your goals and what you did to reach them, for instance, sending resumes, setting up interviews, and interviewing. Track your progress to determine where you need to adjust what you are doing and where you have been successful. Keep yourself motivated and committed. Enlist help from your support system when your enthusiasm lags.

INDEX